STIRLING COUNCIL LIBRARIES

3804802 110694 8

D0191634

Great
Gluten-Free Baking

Great Gluten-Free Baking

over 80 delicious cakes and bakes

Louise Blair

hamlyn

An Hachette UK company
www.hachette.co.uk

First published in Great Britain in 2007 by
Hamlyn, a division of Octopus Publishing Group Ltd
Endeavour House, 189 Shaftesbury Avenue, London WC2H 8JY
www.octopusbooks.co.uk

This edition published in 2015

Copyright © Octopus Publishing Group Ltd 2007, 2015

All rights reserved. No part of this work may be reproduced or utilized
in any form or by any means, electronic or mechanical, including photocopying,
recording or by any information storage and retrieval system, without the prior
written permission of the publisher.

Louise Blair asserts the moral right to be identified as the author of this work.

ISBN 978-0-600-63034-0

A CIP catalogue record for this book is available from the British Library.

Printed and bound in China

10 9 8 7 6 5 4 3 2 1

Notes
Both metric and imperial measurements have been given in all recipes.
Use one set of measurements only, and not a mixture of both.

Standard level spoon measurements are used in all recipes.
1 tablespoon = one 15 ml spoon
1 teaspoon = one 5 ml spoon
All eggs used in the recipe are large.

Ovens should be pre-heated to the specified temperature – if using a fan-assisted
oven, follow the manufacturer's instructions for adjusting the time
and the temperature.

This book includes dishes made with nuts and nut derivatives. It is advisable for
those with known allergic reactions to nuts and nut derivatives and those who may
be potentially vulnerable to these allergies, such as pregnant and nursing mothers,
invalids, the elderly, babies and children, to avoid foods made with nuts. It is also
prudent to check the labels of pre-prepared ingredients for the possible inclusion
of nut derivatives.

This book should not be considered a replacement for professional medical
treatment; a physician should be consulted on all matters relating to health.
While the advice and information in this book are believed to be accurate, neither
the author nor the publisher can accept any legal responsibility for any illness
sustained while following the advice in this book.

Coeliac UK is dedicated to improving the lives of people with coeliac disease
and dermatitis herpetiformis through campaigns, support and research.

Coeliac UK
3rd Floor, Apollo Centre
Desborough Road
High Wycombe
Bucks HP11 2QW

Helpline: 0845 305 2060
www.coeliac.org.uk

contents

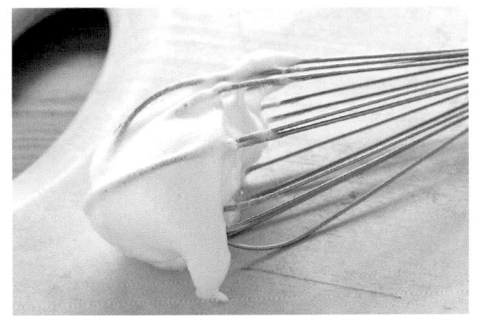

introduction
6

muffins and more
14

family favourites
38

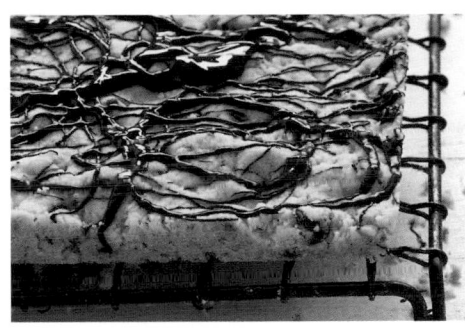

tempting tray bakes
and biscuits
66

something savoury
92

kids in the kitchen
116

index 142

acknowledgements 144

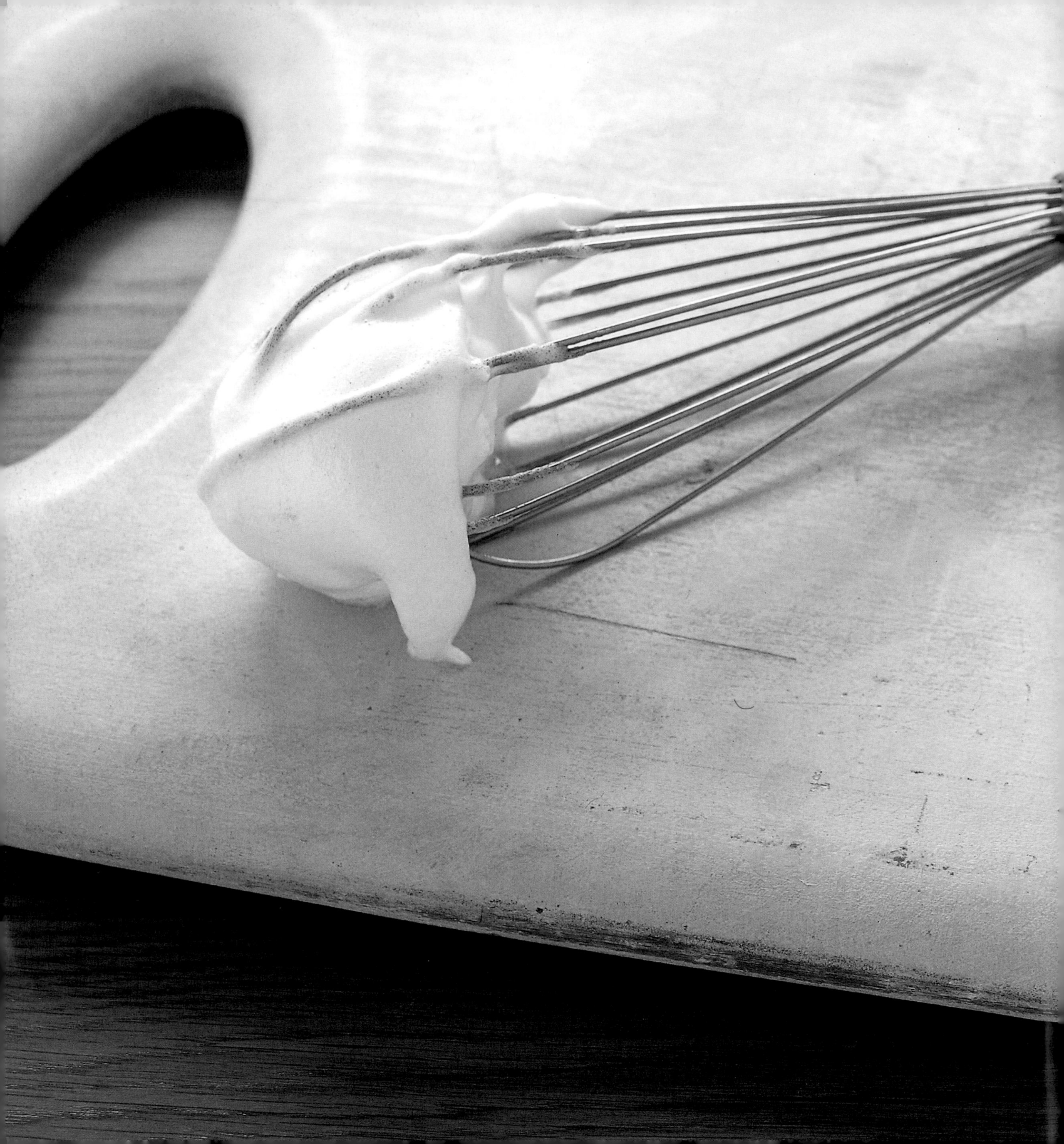

introduction

understanding gluten intolerance and coeliac disease

When our ancestors turned from hunting and gathering to agriculture, gluten-containing crops like wheat and barley were cultivated for the first time. Ever since this evolutionary development some people have been unable to tolerate any gluten in their diet. Initially, sufferers were found only among the groups of people who grew these crops, and much of the world's population remained relatively unaffected. Now, however, as populations have migrated and intermingled, the genetic potential for an intolerance to gluten has increased. The condition arising from this gluten intolerance is called coeliac disease. Research has now shown that a surprisingly high number of people are affected by the disease.

what is gluten?

Gluten is a type of protein found in wheat, barley and rye. It makes up about 80 per cent of the proteins contained in wheat. The gluten in wheat is called gliadin, in barley it is hordein and in rye it is secalin.

Oats contain a protein that is similar to gluten and which is tolerated by most people with coeliac disease. However, as most oats and oat products are contaminated by wheat and barley – either from growing adjacent to these crops and/or from shared milling equipment – it is essential that only pure sources are eaten. You should refer to your healthcare team for specific advice about individual tolerance to oats.

coeliac disease

Coeliac disease is a chronic inflammatory disease of the lining of the small bowel. It is an autoimmune disease that is caused by intolerance to gluten. When gluten is eaten by people with coeliac disease it causes the body's immune system to attack the lining of the gut. The villi (small finger-like projections in the gut which help with absorption) are destroyed. This reduces the ability of the gut to absorb nutrients from food, which can result in vitamin and mineral deficiencies.

Coeliac disease affects one in one hundred people but as it tends to run in families the risk in families with a history of it is increased to one in ten. People of any age, sex or ethnicity can be affected: the most common age of diagnosis is 40–50 years old. Left untreated, it can have serious health implications, such as anaemia, osteoporosis and even some forms of cancer.

Symptoms The symptoms of coeliac disease range in severity from one person to another. Bowel problems such as diarrhoea, constipation, bloating, wind and nausea can be common and are often confused with irritable bowel syndrome (IBS). Other symptoms include an itchy skin rash called dermatitis herpetiformis; weight loss or failure to gain weight, anaemia, tiredness, mouth ulcers, hair loss and depression. Symptoms of coeliac disease are often attributed to stress, resulting in delayed diagnosis or even mis-diagnosis. However, it is now possible to diagnose the disease via simple blood tests in addition to an endoscopy and a biopsy in the jejunal region of the gut.

Treatment The only effective treatment for coeliac disease is to avoid eating gluten permanently. The gut of a person with coeliac disease has often been damaged, over a long period of time, by ingesting gluten. Fortunately, the damage is reversible. Switching to a lifelong gluten-free diet initiates the gut-healing process and, although this can take up to two years or even longer, most people do start to feel better within just a few weeks.

One drawback to a gluten-free diet is that it can be low in fibre, which can lead to constipation in some people. To avoid this it is important to eat plenty of high-fibre, gluten-free foods such as fruit, vegetables and pulses.

living with gluten intolerance

Having an intolerance to gluten needn't mean missing out on your favourite foods. It simply means knowing how to avoid the offending grains and their products, most notably flour, and the substitutions you should make. As well as occurring in obvious foods such as bread, biscuits, cakes, pastries and pasta, it is used in a variety of processed foods, some of them surprising, like tomato sauce, mustard, soups and flavoured potato crisps. Although wheat flour is found in many everyday foods, there are plenty of alternatives nowadays made with gluten-free ingredients. Gluten-free flour and other gluten-free ingredients (see pages 10–13) are widely available from supermarkets or by prescription from your doctor, ensuring gluten-free baking is not only possible, but easy and delicious, as the recipes in this book demonstrate.

gluten-free baking

Making cakes, biscuits, bread and pastry without using wheat flour is perfectly possible. There are many gluten-free baking ingredients available – from pharmacies, healthfood shops, organic food shops, specialist mail order companies and supermarkets – so don't be afraid of trying your hand at some gluten-free baking. Flour aside, many ingredients used in baking are naturally gluten-free, for example milk, eggs, butter, margarine, sugar, fruits, nuts, seeds, vegetables and most preserves and spreads.

using flour

On a gluten-free diet you need to avoid all types of wheat, barley and rye flours. The baking qualities of gluten-free flours are different from wheat flour so there may be some trial and error involved while you become accustomed to cooking with them.

Gluten-free flours can be made from maize/corn, rice, potato, soya, chestnut, buckwheat, millet, gram/chickpea/channa, tapioca and sorghum. You can also use proprietary flour mixes made from a combination of gluten-free ingredients.

Baking without gluten is challenging because removing gluten from flour reduces its elasticity. However, there are some ingredients that can help.

Mix and match gluten-free flours for great results

Xanthan gum Xanthan gum (also known as E415) is a type of starch which is very useful in gluten-free baking as it replaces the 'stretch factor' of gluten, thereby helping gluten-free flours to bind in a way more similar to wheat flour. Xanthan gum comes as a powder and needs to be combined with the gluten-free flour mix before any liquid is added. It can be purchased from health stores.

Guar gum This is a gum derived from the seeds of the locust bean, which acts as a thickening and bulking agent.

shopping for gluten-free ingredients

Not only is home cooking satisfying and usually more tasty than shop-bought products, you'll be confident in the knowledge that your cooking is completely gluten-free as long as you take care when choosing your ingredients. For example, a flour like gram flour (made from pulses) is naturally gluten-free, but it may have been contaminated by traces of gluten-containing wheat flour if milled in the same place or stored in the same containers. It's therefore important to buy reputable brands that can guarantee their products are safe and free from gluten contamination.

Manufacturers now have to list all the ingredients in their products on the food label so you can easily pick out foods that are unsuitable as gluten-containing ingredients will be clearly flagged up.

Just as with standard manufactured foods, the taste and texture of gluten-free foods varies from one brand to another so shop around until you discover the ones that you like. There are plenty of specialist food manufacturers and no shortage of information on them and their products on the Internet. Many offer a mail order service so you can still buy gluten-free foods even if you can't find the products in your local shops. So there's simply no excuse not to buy gluten-free ingredients and get baking! Have fun with the recipes in this book and enjoy making and eating gluten-free cakes, muffins, scones, cookies and breads.

muffins
and more

orange and pistachio butterfly cakes

Orange and pistachio marry so well in these flavoursome cakes.

Makes 12 cakes
Preparation time 10 minutes
Cooking time 15 minutes

150 g (5 oz) rice flour
2 teaspoons gluten-free baking powder
125 g (4 oz) butter, softened
125 g (4 oz) caster sugar
25 g (1 oz) unsalted pistachios, ground
2 large eggs
grated rind and juice 1 orange
4 tablespoons gluten-free orange curd

Nutritional information:
Kcals 196 (819 kj) Protein 3 g Carb 23 g
Fat 10 g Saturated fat 6 g Fibre 1 g

1 Line a 12-hole bun tin with paper cases. Place all the ingredients apart from the orange curd in a food processor and whiz until smooth, or beat in a large bowl.

2 Divide the mixture between the paper cases and place in a preheated oven, 200°C (400°F) Gas Mark 6, for 12–15 minutes until golden and firm to the touch. Remove the cakes from the oven and transfer to a wire rack to cool.

3 Cut the top off each bun to give a level surface, giving you 12 flattened cone-shaped pieces of cake. Spread the tops with a little orange curd, then cut the cones in half and place on top at an angle to resemble butterfly wings.

date and pecan muffins

The dates provide a richness of flavour and the pecans a satisfying crunch, making these muffins quite delicious.

Makes 18 muffins
Preparation time 10 minutes
Cooking time 20 minutes

100 g (3½ oz) ready-to-eat dried dates, chopped
2 teaspoons bicarbonate of soda
2 tablespoons boiling water
400 g (13 oz) brown rice flour
1 tablespoon gluten-free baking powder
100 g (3½ oz) soft dark brown sugar
100 g (3½ oz) pecans, roughly chopped
100 g (3½ oz) butter, melted
4 eggs, beaten
300 ml (½ pint) buttermilk
2 tablespoons milk
2 tablespoons demerara sugar

Nutritional information:
Kcals 212 (886 kj) Protein 6 g Carb 25 g
Fat 10 g Saturated fat 4 g Fibre 3 g

1 Line two large 12-hole muffin trays with 18 large muffin cases. Place the dates, bicarbonate of soda and water in a bowl and set aside for 10 minutes.

2 Meanwhile, in a large bowl, mix together the flour, baking powder, dark brown sugar and pecans. In another bowl, mix together the butter, eggs, buttermilk and milk, then pour this into the dry mixture along with the dates and their liquid and give a quick stir just to combine all the ingredients roughly.

3 Spoon the mixture into the muffin tins, sprinkle over a little demerara sugar, and place in a preheated oven, 200°C (400°F) Gas Mark 6, for 15–20 minutes until golden and risen. Remove the muffins from the oven and transfer to a wire rack to cool.

lavender fairy cakes

The lavender makes these little cakes perfect for sophisticated tea-time entertaining.

Makes 12 cakes
Preparation time 10 minutes
Cooking time 15 minutes

1 tablespoon milk
1 teaspoon lavender flowers (the small, individual flowerheads, removed from the stalk)
125 g (4 oz) caster sugar
100 g (3½ oz) butter, softened
100 g (3½ oz) rice flour
1 tablespoon chickpea/gram flour
2 eggs, beaten
2 tablespoons ground almonds
1 teaspoon gluten-free baking powder
1 teaspoon xanthan gum

for the decoration
125 g (4 oz) icing sugar
12 small lavender heads

Nutritional information:
Kcals 185 (773 kj) **Protein** 2 g **Carb** 27 g
Fat 8 g **Saturated fat** 5 g **Fibre** 1 g

1 Line a 12-hole bun tin with paper cases. Place the milk and lavender in a ramekin, cover with clingfilm and microwave on full power for 10 seconds. Remove and leave for 10 minutes to allow the flavours to develop.

2 Place all the cake ingredients, including the lavender-infused milk, in a food processor and whiz until smooth, or beat in a large bowl.

3 Spoon the mixture into the paper cases and place in a preheated oven, 180°C (350°F) Gas Mark 4, for 12–15 minutes until golden and just firm to the touch. Remove the cakes from the oven and transfer to a wire rack to cool.

4 Add a few drops of water to the icing sugar – just enough to give a stiff icing. Smooth a little over each bun and decorate with a lavender head.

plum and polenta muffins

These unusual muffins are great for picnics
or afternoon snacks.

Makes 12 muffins
Preparation time 20 minutes
Cooking time 20 minutes

200 g (7 oz) ripe plums, stoned and
    roughly chopped
200 g (7 oz) soft light brown sugar
50 g (2 oz) brown rice flour
50 g (2 oz) maize flour
2 teaspoons gluten-free baking powder
1 teaspoon xanthan gum
1 teaspoon ground cinnamon
100 g (3½ oz) polenta
2 eggs, beaten
few drops vanilla extract
75 g (3 oz) butter, melted
200 ml (7 fl oz) buttermilk

Nutritional information:
Kcals 227 (949 kj) Protein 4 g Carb 33 g
Fat 9 g Saturated fat 4 g Fibre 1 g

1 Line a large 12-hole muffin tray with large muffin cases. Place the plums in a bowl and sprinkle over a little of the sugar and set aside for 10 minutes until the juices begin to ooze.

2 Meanwhile, place all the dry ingredients in a large bowl and stir together. Combine the eggs, vanilla extract, butter and buttermilk in another bowl, then stir this into the dry ingredients along with the plums and any juices.

3 Spoon the mixture into the paper cases and place in a preheated oven, 180°C (350°F) Gas Mark 4, for 20 minutes until risen and golden. Remove the muffins from the oven and transfer to a wire rack to cool.

white chocolate and apricot muffins

Melting white chocolate and squishy apricots are very moreish, so these muffins won't last long.

Makes 15 muffins
Preparation time 10 minutes
Cooking time 20 minutes

100 g (3½ oz) ready-to-eat dried
    apricots, chopped
grated rind and juice 1 orange
400 g (13 oz) brown rice flour
1 teaspoon bicarbonate of soda
2 teaspoons gluten-free baking powder
125 g (4 oz) golden caster sugar
75 g (3 oz) gluten free white chocolate,
    chopped
75 g (3 oz) butter, melted
4 eggs, beaten
300 ml (½ pint) buttermilk

Nutritional information:
Kcals 227 (949 kj) Protein 4 g Carb 33 g
Fat 9 g Saturated fat 6 g Fibre 2 g

1 Line two large 12-hole muffin trays with 15 large muffin cases. Place the apricots, orange rind and juice in a small saucepan, bring to the boil and simmer gently for 5 minutes, then set aside.

2 Meanwhile, sift the flour, bicarbonate of soda and baking powder together into a large bowl. Add the sugar and chocolate and stir together. Mix together the wet ingredients and the soaked apricots and fold them roughly into the dry mixture.

3 Spoon the mixture into the paper cases and and place in a preheated oven, 180°C (350°F) Gas Mark 4, for 20 minutes until well risen and golden. Remove the muffins from the oven and transfer to a wire rack to cool.

lemon and raspberry cupcakes

These luscious melt-in-the-mouth cakes combine the sweetness of raspberries with the sharpness of lemon.

Makes 12 cakes
Preparation time 10 minutes
Cooking time 15 minutes

150 g (5 oz) butter, softened
150 g (5 oz) granulated sugar
75 g (3 oz) rice flour
75 g (3 oz) maize/cornflour
1 tablespoon gluten-free baking powder
grated rind and juice 1 lemon
3 eggs, beaten
125 g (4 oz) raspberries
1 tablespoon gluten-free lemon curd

Nutritional information:
Kcals 206 (861 kj) Protein 3 g Carb 22 g
Fat 12 g Saturated fat 7 g Fibre 1 g

1 Line a large 12-hole muffin tray with large muffin cases. Place all the ingredients except the raspberries and the lemon curd in a large bowl and whisk together using an electric hand whisk or beat with a wooden spoon. Fold in the raspberries.

2 Spoon half of the mixture into the paper cases, dot over a little lemon curd, then add the remaining sponge mixture. Place in a preheated oven, 200°C (400°F) Gas Mark 6, for 12–15 minutes until golden and firm to the touch. Remove the cakes from the oven and transfer to a wire rack to cool.

chocolate courgette muffins

Grated courgettes are the secret to keeping these muffins light and moist.

Makes 12 muffins
Preparation time 10 minutes
Cooking time 20 minutes

2 medium courgettes, grated
2 eggs, beaten
100 g (3½ oz) vegetable oil
125 g (4 oz) caster sugar
75 g (3 oz) ready-to-eat dried dates,
   chopped
2 tablespoons milk
100 g (3½ oz) maize/cornflour
125 g (4 oz) brown rice flour
2 tablespoons cocoa powder
1 teaspoon xanthan gum
2 teaspoons gluten-free baking powder

for the topping (if desired)
250 g (8 oz) quark
1 tablespoon icing sugar
grated rind 1 orange
few toasted chopped nuts (optional)

Nutritional information:
Kcals 223 (932 kj) Protein 7 g Carb 28 g
Fat 10 g Saturated fat 2 g Fibre 2 g

SHOWN ON PAGES 14–15

1 Line a large 12-hole muffin tray with large muffin cases. (If you use coloured cases as pictured on pages 14–15 the dark muffin will show through, so you can achieve a particularly attractive effect if you line each hole with two or more coloured cases.) Place the courgettes, eggs, oil, sugar, dates and milk in a large bowl and stir together. In a separate bowl, sift together the dry ingredients then quickly and roughly stir them into the wet ingredients.

2 Divide the mixture between the muffin cases and place in a preheated oven, 180°C (350°F) Gas Mark 4, for about 20 minutes until risen and firm to the touch. Remove the muffins from the oven and transfer to a wire rack to cool.

3 For an extra special treat, place the quark, icing sugar and orange rind in a bowl and beat together, then smooth the topping over the muffins. Sprinkle with a few nuts, if using.

cranberry and orange cupcakes

With their seasonal flavours, these little cakes are
great at Christmas for a change from fruit cake.

Makes 12 cakes
Preparation time 10 minutes
Cooking time 15 minutes

125 g (4 oz) dried cranberries
grated rind and juice 1 orange
150 g (5 oz) butter, softened
150 g (5 oz) granulated sugar
75 g (3 oz) rice flour
75 g (3 oz) maize/cornflour
1 tablespoon gluten-free baking powder
2 tablespoons milk
3 eggs, beaten

for the icing
200 g (7 oz) icing sugar
grated rind and juice 1 small orange

Nutritional information:
Kcals 265 (1108 kj) Protein 4 g Carb 36 g
Fat 12 g Saturated fat 7 g Fibre 2 g

1 Line a 12-hole bun tin with paper cases. Place the cranberries
and orange rind and juice in a small pan, bring to the boil then
simmer gently for 5 minutes.

2 Meanwhile, place the remaining cake ingredients in a food
processor and whiz until smooth (or beat in a large bowl). Add
the cranberries and any juice and stir the ingredients together, then
spoon into the paper cases. Place in a preheated oven, 200°C (400°F)
Gas Mark 6, for 12–15 minutes until golden and risen. Remove the
cakes from the oven and transfer to a wire rack to cool.

3 In a small bowl, mix together the icing sugar, grated rind and
enough orange juice to make a thickish icing. Smooth a little
over the cakes and leave to set.

cherry crumble muffins

Juicy cherries keep these muffins really moist, while the crumble topping adds some crunch.

Makes 12 muffins
Preparation time 10 minutes
Cooking time 20 minutes

250 g (8 oz) brown rice flour
1 teaspoon bicarbonate of soda
2 teaspoon gluten-free baking powder
125 g (4 oz) golden caster sugar
1 x 300 g (10 oz) can black cherries, drained
75 g (3 oz) butter, melted
2 eggs, beaten
150 ml (¼ pint) buttermilk

for the crumbly topping
1 tablespoon ground almonds
1 tablespoon soft light brown sugar
1 tablespoon brown rice flour
1 tablespoon butter

Nutritional information:
Kcals 189 (790 kj) Protein 3 g Carb 27 g
Fat 8 g Saturated fat 5 g Fibre 1 g

1 Line a large 12-hole muffin tray with large muffin cases. Sift the flour, bicarbonate of soda and baking powder together in a large bowl, then stir in the sugar.

2 In a separate bowl, mix together the cherries, butter, eggs and buttermilk. Gently combine the dry and wet ingredients, then spoon the mixture into the muffin cases.

3 Quickly rub together the topping ingredients and sprinkle over the muffin mixture, then place the muffins in a preheated oven, 180°C (350°F) Gas Mark 4, for 20 minutes until golden and risen. Remove the muffins from the oven and cool on a wire rack.

tiramisu cupcakes

The combination of coffee and marsala provides a
taste of Italy in these little cakes.

Makes 12 cakes
Preparation time 10 minutes
Cooking time 15 minutes

150 g (5 oz) butter, softened
150 g (5 oz) granulated sugar
75 g (3 oz) rice flour
75 g (3 oz) maize/cornflour
1 tablespoon cocoa powder
1 tablespoon gluten-free baking powder
1 teaspoon instant espresso
2 tablespoons milk
3 eggs, beaten

for the topping
250 g (8 oz) mascarpone cheese
2 tablespoons icing sugar
1 tablespoon marsala

Nutritional information:
Kcals 276 (1154 kj) **Protein** 4 g **Carb** 21 g
Fat 20 g **Saturated fat** 12 g **Fibre** 1 g

1 Line a 12-hole bun tin with paper cases. Place all the cake
ingredients in a food processor and whiz until smooth, or beat
in a large bowl.

2 Spoon the mixture into the paper cases and and place in a
preheated oven, 200°C (400°F) Gas Mark 6, for 12–15 minutes
until risen. Remove the cakes from the oven and transfer to a wire
rack to cool.

3 Place the topping ingredients in a bowl and beat together, then
smooth a little mixture over each cake.

coconut buns

These are really moist and flavoursome – delicious with a cup of tea at any time of day.

Makes 12 buns
Preparation time 10 minutes
Cooking time 15 minutes

175 g (6 oz) butter, softened
175 g (6 oz) caster sugar
few drops vanilla extract
3 eggs, beaten
100 g (3½ oz) brown rice flour
100 g (3½ oz) maize/cornflour
2 teaspoons gluten-free baking powder
50 g (2 oz) desiccated coconut soaked in
   100 ml (3½ fl oz) boiling water

for the topping
50 g (2 oz) butter, softened
100 g (3½ oz) icing sugar
2 tablespoons desiccated coconut,
   toasted

Nutritional information:
Kcals 323 (1350 kj) **Protein** 2 g **Carb** 37 g
Fat 19 g **Saturated fat** 13 g **Fibre** 1 g

1 Line a 12-hole bun tin with paper cases. Place all the bun ingredients in a food processor and whiz until smooth, or beat in a large bowl.

2 Spoon the mixture into the paper cases and place in a preheated oven, 180°C (350°F) Gas Mark 4, for 12–15 minutes until golden and risen. Remove the buns from the oven and transfer to a wire rack to cool.

3 Place the butter and icing sugar in a bowl and beat together until pale and creamy, then stir in the toasted coconut. Spread a little icing on each bun.

scrumptious strawberry scones

No one would guess that these light and airy scones are gluten free.

Makes 8 scones
Preparation time 10 minutes
Cooking time 12 minutes

175 g (6 oz) rice flour, plus a little extra for dusting
75 g (3 oz) potato flour
1 teaspoon xanthan gum
1 teaspoon gluten-free baking powder
1 teaspoon bicarbonate of soda
75 g (3 oz) butter, cubed
40 g (1½ oz) caster sugar
1 large egg, beaten
3 tablespoons buttermilk, plus a little extra for brushing

for the filling
142 ml (¼ pint) carton double cream
250 g (8 oz) strawberries, lightly crushed

Nutritional information:
Kcals 292 (1221 kj) Protein 5 g Carb 30 g
Fat 17 g Saturated fat 10 g Fibre 2 g

1 Place the flours, xanthan gum, baking powder, bicarbonate of soda and butter in a food processor and whiz until the mixture resembles fine breadcrumbs, or rub in by hand in a large bowl. Stir in the sugar. Using the blade of a knife, stir in the egg and buttermilk until the mixture comes together.

2 Tip the dough out on to a surface dusted lightly with rice flour and gently press it down to a thickness of 2.5 cm (1 inch). Using a 5-cm (2-inch) cutter, cut out eight scones. Place on a lightly floured baking sheet, brush with a little buttermilk and then place in a preheated oven, 220°C (425°F) Gas Mark 7, for about 12 minutes until golden and risen. Remove the scones from the oven and transfer to a wire rack to cool.

3 Meanwhile, whisk the cream until it forms fairly firm peaks and fold the strawberries into it. Split the scones in half and fill with the strawberry cream. Scones are best served on the day they are cooked, preferably still just warm.

moist orange buns

Use lemon in place of orange in these buns if you prefer a sharper citrus taste.

Makes 18 buns
Preparation time 10 minutes
Cooking time 15 minutes

200 g (7 oz) butter, softened
200 g (7 oz) golden caster sugar
3 eggs, beaten
40 g (1½ oz) brown rice flour
200 g (7 oz) ground almonds
grated rind and juice 1 orange
50 g (2 oz) flaked almonds

Nutritional information:
Kcals 225 (940 kj) Protein 4 g Carb 12 g
Fat 18 g Saturated fat 7 g Fibre 1 g

1 Line two mini 12-hole bun tins with 18 mini paper cases. Place the butter and sugar in a large bowl and beat together until pale and creamy. Gradually beat in the eggs, then fold the flour, ground almonds and orange rind and juice into the mixture.

2 Spoon the mixture into the paper cases, sprinkle over the almonds and place in a preheated oven, 180°C (350°F) Gas Mark 4, for 12–15 minutes until golden and risen. Remove the buns from the oven and transfer to a wire rack to cool.

bite-sized mince pies

The cream cheese in these mini mince pies makes them wonderfully moist.

Makes 18 pies
Preparation time 15 minutes, plus chilling
Cooking time 15 minutes

75 g (3 oz) polenta
75 g (3 oz) rice flour, plus a little extra for dusting
½ teaspoon xanthan gum
good pinch mixed spice
grated rind 1 lemon or orange
100 g (3½ oz) butter
1 tablespoon golden caster sugar
1 egg, beaten
a little milk for brushing
a little icing sugar for dusting

for the filling
450 g (1 lb) jar gluten-free mincemeat
100 g (3½ oz) cream cheese

Nutritional information:
Kcals 122 (510 kj) Protein 1 g Carb 16 g
Fat 6 g Saturated fat 4 g Fibre 1 g

1 Place the polenta, flour, xanthan gum, spice, lemon rind, butter and sugar in a food processor and whiz until it resembles fine breadcrumbs, or rub in by hand in a large bowl. Add the egg and very gently mix in using a knife, adding a little cold water if the mixture is too dry. Bring the mixture together to form a ball, wrap closely and chill for 30 minutes.

2 Remove the pastry from the refrigerator and knead it on a surface dusted lightly with rice flour to soften it a little. Then roll it out thinly and cut out 18 x 5-cm (2-inch) rounds and the same number of slightly smaller lids. Use the larger circles to line 18 holes in two 12-hole mini tart tins.

3 Spoon a little mincemeat and a little cream cheese on to each pastry base, brush the rim of the lids with milk so they stick to the bases and put them in place, pressing lightly to seal. Brush the tops with a little extra milk and place in a preheated oven, 200°C (400°F) Gas Mark 6, for 12–15 minutes until golden. Remove the pies from the oven and transfer to a wire rack to cool a little, then serve warm, dusted with icing sugar.

perfect
pecan pies

The ideal entertaining pud! Serve with crème fraîche
or some gluten-free ice cream for a treat.

Makes 8 pies
Preparation time 15 minutes, plus
  chilling
Cooking time 20 minutes

**75 g (3 oz) brown rice flour, plus a little
  extra for dusting**
50 g (2 oz) chickpea/gram flour
75 g (3 oz) polenta
1 teaspoon xanthan gum
125 g (4 oz) butter, cubed
2 tablespoons caster sugar
1 egg, beaten

for the filling
100 g (3½ oz) light muscovado sugar
150 g (5 oz) butter
125 g (4 oz) honey
**175 g (6 oz) pecan halves, half of them
  roughly chopped**
2 eggs, beaten

Nutritional information:
Kcals 606 (2533 kj) Protein 7 g Carb 43 g
Fat 46 g Saturated fat 21 g Fibre 2 g

1 Place the flours, polenta, xanthan gum and butter in a food processor and whiz until the mixture resembles fine breadcrumbs, or rub in by hand in a large bowl. Stir in the sugar. Add the egg and very gently mix in using a knife, adding enough cold water (probably a couple of teaspoons) to make a dough. Try not to let it become too wet. Knead for a couple of minutes, then wrap closely in clingfilm and chill for about an hour.

2 Meanwhile, place the sugar, butter and honey for the filling in a medium saucepan and heat until the sugar has dissolved. Leave to cool for 10 minutes.

3 While the filling is cooling, remove the dough from the refrigerator and knead it on a surface dusted lightly with rice flour to soften it a little. Divide the dough into eight then roll each piece out to a thickness of 2.5 mm (⅛ inch). Use to line eight individual 11.5-cm (4½-inch) pie tins, rolling the rolling pin over the top to cut off the excess dough.

4 Stir the chopped pecans and eggs into the filling mixture and pour into the pastry-lined tins. Arrange the pecan halves over the top, then place the tins in a preheated oven, 200°C (400°F) Gas Mark 6, for 15–20 minutes until the filling is firm. Remove the pies and leave to cool.

banoffee bites

The popular combination of banana and toffee makes these little cakes absolutely delicious!

Makes 24 bites
Preparation time 10 minutes
Cooking time 12 minutes

200 g (7 oz) brown rice flour
75 g (3 oz) butter, softened
75 g (3 oz) golden caster sugar
2 teaspoons gluten-free baking powder
1 large banana, mashed
2 eggs
6 toffees, chopped

for the topping
15 g (½ oz) chewy banana slices or
   dried banana chips
1 tablespoon light muscovado sugar

Nutritional information:
Kcals 122 (510 kj) Protein 1 g Carb 16 g
Fat 6 g Saturated fat 4 g Fibre 1 g

1 Line two 12-hole mini bun tins with paper cases. Place all the cake ingredients except the toffees in a food processor and whiz until smooth, or beat in a large bowl, then stir in the toffees.

2 Spoon the mixture into the paper cases, sprinkle over most of the muscovado sugar and place in a preheated oven, 200°C (400°F) Gas Mark 6, for 10–12 minutes until golden and just firm to the touch. Remove the cakes from the oven and cool on a wire rack. Top with chewy banana slices or banana chips and sprinkle with the remaining sugar, if wished.

family favourites

blueberry and apple cake

This moist upside-down cake is so easy to make and is delicious served with a little crème fraîche.

Serves 12
Preparation time 10 minutes
Cooking time 1 hour

2 small eating apples, peeled, cored and sliced
250 g (8 oz) butter, softened
250 g (8 oz) caster sugar
250 g (8 oz) rice flour
1 tablespoon gluten-free baking powder
4 eggs
150 g (5 oz) blueberries

Nutritional information:
Kcals 312 (1304 kj) **Protein** 5 g **Carb** 35 g
Fat 17 g **Saturated fat** 11 g **Fibre** 2 g

1 Grease and line the base of a 23-cm (9-inch) loose-bottomed deep cake tin. Layer the apples over the base of the cake tin.

2 Place the butter, sugar, flour, baking powder and eggs in a food processor and whiz for 30 seconds or until well combined, or beat in a large bowl. Add the blueberries and whiz for 5 seconds until roughly chopped or stir until mixed in well.

3 Spoon the mixture over the apples. Place in a preheated oven, 200°C (400°F) Gas Mark 6, for 50–60 minutes until golden and just firm to the touch. Remove the cake from the oven, cool for 10 minutes in the tin then turn out on to a wire rack with the apples on top to cool completely.

chocolate hazelnut cake

This light and airy cake makes a decadent dessert
with a scoop of gluten-free ice cream or crème fraîche.

Serves 12
Preparation time 15 minutes
Cooking time 40 minutes

250 g (8 oz) blanched hazelnuts
6 eggs, separated
200 g (7 oz) icing sugar, sifted
75 g (3 oz) gluten-free breadcrumbs
1 tablespoon cocoa powder
grated rind and juice 1 orange
75 g (3 oz) butter, melted

Nutritional information:
Kcals 295 (1233 kj) Protein 7 g Carb 22 g
Fat 20 g Saturated fat 5 g Fibre 2 g

1 Grease and line a 23-cm (9-inch) deep spring-form tin. Place the hazelnuts on a baking sheet and cook in a preheated oven, 180°C (350°F) Gas Mark 4, for 10 minutes until golden. Allow to cool a little, then place in a food processor or liquidizer and whiz until they resemble fine breadcrumbs.

2 Place the egg whites in a large clean bowl and whisk until they form stiff peaks. Add 2 tablespoons of the icing sugar and continue to whisk until thick.

3 Place the egg yolks in a separate bowl with the remaining icing sugar and whisk until pale. Fold in the remaining ingredients, including the egg whites, then transfer to the prepared tin. Place in the oven for 40 minutes, then remove the cake from the oven and transfer to a wire rack to cool.

coconut and mango cake

This delicious tropical-inspired cake is great for summer entertaining.

Serves 12
Preparation time 10 minutes
Cooking time 50 minutes

100 g (3½ oz) butter, softened
100 g (3½ oz) soft light brown sugar
4 eggs, separated
400 ml (14 fl oz) buttermilk
200 g (7 oz) polenta
200 g (7 oz) rice flour
2 teaspoons gluten-free baking powder
50 g (2 oz) coconut milk powder
50 g (2 oz) desiccated coconut
flesh 1 ripe mango, puréed

for the filling
250 g (8 oz) mascarpone cheese
flesh 1 ripe mango, finely chopped
2 tablespoons icing sugar

Nutritional information:
Kcals 374 (1563 kj) Protein 9 g Carb 37 g
Fat 22 g Saturated fat 13 g Fibre 3 g

1 Grease and line a 23-cm (9-inch) round deep cake tin. Place the butter and sugar in a large bowl and beat until light and fluffy, then beat in the egg yolks, buttermilk, polenta flour, baking powder, coconut milk powder and desiccated coconut. In a large clean bowl, whisk the egg whites until they form soft peaks, then fold into the cake mixture with the puréed mango.

2 Spoon the mixture into the prepared tin and place in a preheated oven, 200°C (400°F) Gas Mark 6, for 45–50 minutes until golden and firm to the touch. Remove the cake from the oven and transfer to a wire rack to cool.

3 When the cake is cool, slice it in half. Place the filling ingredients in a bowl and beat together. Use half the filling to sandwich the cake together then smooth the remaining mixture over the top.

fudgy apple loaf

Gooey fudge and moist apple makes this loaf a real family favourite.

Serves 12
Preparation time 25 minutes
Cooking time 1½ hours

250 g (8 oz) caster sugar
3 eggs
400 g (13 oz) brown rice flour
1 teaspoon gluten-free baking powder
200 g (7 oz) butter, melted
few drops vanilla essence
2 eating apples, peeled, cored and
   chopped

for the fudge
397 g (13 oz) can condensed milk
150 ml (¼ pint) milk
500 g (1 lb) soft light brown sugar
100 g (3½ oz) butter

Nutritional information:
Kcals 376 (1572 kj) **Protein** 2 g **Carb** 57 g
Fat 16 g **Saturated fat** 11 g **Fibre** 0 g

1 To make the fudge, place all the ingredients in a heavy-based saucepan, heat gently until the sugar has dissolved, bring to the boil and boil for about 10 minutes until the mixture reaches 116°C (230°F) on a sugar thermometer. Remove from the heat and beat for 5 minutes, then pour into a tin and set aside to cool.

2 Grease and line a 900-g (2-lb) loaf tin. Place the sugar and eggs in a large bowl and whisk together until pale and thick. Sift the flour and baking powder into the mixture together, then fold it in with the butter, vanilla essence, two thirds of the apple and 75 g (3 oz) of the fudge, chopped. Spoon into the prepared tin, then scatter over the remaining apple and a further 25 g (1 oz) of chopped fudge.

3 Place in a preheated oven, 180°C (350°F) Gas Mark 4, for about 1½ hours until golden and firm to touch. Remove the cake from the oven and transfer to a wire rack to cool.

orange and honey cake

This is great to take on a picnic and serve with some fresh fruit or berries.

Serves 10
Preparation time 10 minutes
Cooking time 1 hour

150 g (5 oz) butter, softened
200 g (7 oz) caster sugar
grated rind and juice 1 orange
2 tablespoons runny honey
3 tablespoons marmalade
3 eggs, beaten
100 g (3½ oz) brown rice flour
1 teaspoon gluten-free baking powder
75 g (3 oz) polenta

Nutritional information:
Kcals 270 (1129 kj) Protein 1 g Carb 41 g
Fat 12 g Saturated fat 8 g Fibre 1 g

1 Grease and line a 20-cm (8-inch) square deep baking tin. Place the butter and sugar in a large bowl, then beat until light and fluffy. Whisk together the orange rind and juice, honey, marmalade and eggs, then beat into the creamed butter mixture, adding a little of the flour if the mixture curdles.

2 Stir in the remaining ingredients, then spoon into the prepared tin and place in a preheated oven, 170°C (325°F) Gas Mark 3, for about 1 hour until just firm in the middle. Remove the cake from the oven and transfer to a wire rack to cool.

chocolate and chestnut roulade

The flavours of chocolate and chestnut work so well together in this moreish pudding/cake.

Serves 8
Preparation time 15 minutes
Cooking time 20 minutes

6 eggs, separated
125 g (4 oz) caster sugar
2 tablespoons cocoa powder
icing sugar, for dusting

for the filling
150 ml (¼ pint) carton whipping cream, whipped
100 g (3½ oz) chestnut purée or sweetened chestnut spread

Nutritional information:
Kcals 215 (899 kj) Protein 6 g Carb 21 g
Fat 12 g Saturated fat 3 g Fibre 1 g

1 Grease and line a 29 x 18-cm (11½ x 7-inch) Swiss roll tin. Place the egg whites in a large clean bowl and whisk until they form soft peaks. Place the egg yolks and sugar in a separate bowl and whisk together until thick and pale. Fold in the cocoa powder and the egg whites, then tip into the prepared tin.

2 Place in a preheated oven, 180°C (350°F) Gas Mark 4, for 20 minutes, then remove from the oven and cool in the tin. Tip out on to a piece of greaseproof paper that has been dusted with icing sugar.

3 Place the cream in a large clean bowl and whisk until it forms soft peaks. Fold the chestnut purée or sweetened chestnut spread into the cream, then smooth the mixture over the roulade.

4 Using the greaseproof paper to help you, carefully roll up the roulade from one short end and lift it gently on to its serving dish. (Don't worry if it cracks: it won't detract from its appearance or taste.) Dust with extra icing sugar. Chill until needed and eat on the day it is made.

butterscotch layer cake

Impress friends and family with this simple but delicious sponge.

Serves 10
Preparation time 10 minutes
Cooking time 25 minutes

250 g (8 oz) unsalted butter, softened
250 g (8 oz) golden caster sugar
4 eggs
250 g (8 oz) rice flour
1 tablespoon gluten-free baking powder
2 tablespoons milk

for the filling
300 g (10 oz) quark
250 g (8 oz) dulce de leche

Nutritional information:
Kcals 444 (1856 kj) Protein 11 g Carb 51 g
Fat 22 g Saturated fat 13 g Fibre 1 g

1 Grease two 20-cm (8-inch) cake tins. Place all the cake ingredients in a food processor and whiz until smooth, or beat in a large bowl. Spoon into the prepared tins and place in a preheated oven, 200°C (400°F) Gas Mark 6, for 20–25 minutes until golden and just firm to the touch. Remove the cakes from the oven and transfer to a wire rack to cool.

2 Place the quark and dulce de leche in a bowl and beat together. Use half the mixture to sandwich the cakes together and half for the topping. Eat on the same day or keep chilled for up to 2 days.

moist almond cake

Ground almonds give this cake a great texture
and flavour.

Serves 10
Preparation time 10 minutes
Cooking time 1 hour 50 minutes

2 large oranges
250 g (8 oz) caster sugar
275 g (9 oz) ground almonds
1 teaspoon gluten-free baking powder
6 eggs
200 g (7 oz) brown rice flour

Nutritional information:
Kcals 371 (1551 kj) Protein 12 g Carb 41 g
Fat 18 g Saturated fat 2 g Fibre 4 g

1 Grease a 20-cm (8-inch) round deep cake tin. Place the oranges in a large pan of water, bring to the boil and simmer gently for 1 hour. Then remove the oranges from the pan, place in a food processor or liquidizer and blend until pulpy. Remove any obvious pips.

2 Add the remaining ingredients and blend until smooth, then pour into the prepared tin and place in a preheated oven, 180°C (350°F) Gas Mark 4, for 45–50 minutes until just firm to touch. Remove the cake from the oven and transfer to a wire rack to cool. Serve with whipped cream, if wanted.

chocolate and rum cake

This may not be a good choice for the calorie conscious,
but it makes a great cake or dinner party dessert.

Serves 16
Preparation time 15 minutes
Cooking time 25 minutes

150 g (5 oz) gluten-free plain chocolate
grated rind and juice 1 orange
few drops rum essence (optional)
150 g (5 oz) unsalted butter, softened
150 g (5 oz) caster sugar
4 eggs, separated
150 g (5 oz) ground almonds

for the chocolate icing
150 g (5 oz) gluten-free plain chocolate
100 g (3½ oz) unsalted butter

for the topping (optional)
8–16 crystallized violet petals

Nutritional information:
Kcals 264 (1102 kj) Protein 4 g Carb 18 g
Fat 20 g Saturated fat 40 g Fibre 0.5 g

1 Grease and line 2 x 20-cm (8-inch) sandwich cake tins. Melt together the chocolate, orange rind and juice and rum essence, if using, in a heatproof bowl over a pan of simmering water.

2 Place the butter and all but 1 tablespoon of the sugar in a large bowl and beat until pale and fluffy. Beat in the egg yolks, one by one, then stir in the melted chocolate.

3 Place the egg whites in a large clean bowl and whisk until they form soft peaks. Add the remaining sugar and continue to whisk until stiff peaks form. Fold the egg whites into the chocolate mixture with the ground almonds, then spoon into the prepared cake tins.

4 Place in a preheated oven, 180°C (350°F) Gas Mark 4, for 20–25 minutes, until the sides are cooked but the centre is still a little unset. Remove the cakes from the oven, leave to cool for a few minutes in the tins then turn out gently on to a wire rack.

5 To ice, melt the chocolate as before then whisk in the butter, a tablespoon at a time, until melted. Remove from the heat and whisk occasionally until cool. If the icing is runny, put the bowl in the refrigerator until it firms up a little. Fill and ice the cooled cake with the chocolate mixture. Top with crystallized violet petals if liked.

pear and marzipan loaf

The combination of sticky pear and melting marzipan
is fabulous in this loaf.

Serves 12
Preparation time 10 minutes, plus
 soaking overnight
Cooking time 1–1½ hours

150 g (5 oz) sultanas
300 g (10 oz) ready-to-eat dried pears,
 chopped
2 tablespoons apple juice
few drops almond essence
275 g (9 oz) white marzipan, cut into
 small cubes and frozen
3 tablespoons ground almonds
75 g (3 oz) golden caster sugar
100 g (3½ oz) butter, softened
2 eggs, beaten
175 g (6 oz) rice flour

Nutritional information:
Kcals 344 (1438 kj) **Protein** 5 g **Carb** 52 g
Fat 13 g **Saturated fat** 5 g **Fibre** 4 g

1 Place the sultanas, pears, apple juice and almond essence in a non-metallic bowl, cover and leave overnight.

2 Grease and line a 900-g (2-lb) loaf tin. Place all the remaining ingredients in a large bowl and beat together, stirring in the soaked fruit until well combined.

3 Spoon the mixture into the prepared tin, then place in a preheated oven, 150°C (300°F) Gas Mark 2, for 1–1½ hours until a skewer inserted in the middle comes out clean. Remove the cake from the oven and transfer to a wire rack to cool.

espresso cream gâteau

This gâteau, which is quick and easy to make, is a great choice for an adult birthday cake.

Serves 10
Preparation time 10 minutes
Cooking time 25 minutes

250 g (8 oz) butter, softened
250 g (8 oz) golden caster sugar
4 eggs
250 g (8 oz) rice flour
2 teaspoons gluten-free baking powder
1 tablespoon instant coffee, dissolved
   in 1 tablespoon boiling water

for the filling and topping
200 ml (7 fl oz) double cream
1 teaspoon instant coffee, dissolved in
   1 teaspoon boiling water
1 tablespoon icing sugar
handful gluten-free chocolate-covered
   coffee beans
1 teaspoon cocoa powder

Nutritional information:
Kcals 452 (1889 kj) Protein 6 g Carb 40 g
Fat 30 g Saturated fat 19 g Fibre 1 g

1 Grease two 20-cm (8-inch) sandwich tins and dust with rice flour. Place all the cake ingredients in a food processor and whiz until smooth, or beat in a large bowl.

2 Spoon the mixture into the prepared tin, then place in a preheated oven, 200°C (400°F) Gas Mark 6, for 20–25 minutes until golden and just firm to the touch. Remove the cake from the oven and transfer to a wire rack to cool.

3 In a large bowl, whisk the cream, coffee and icing sugar until the mixture forms soft peaks. Sandwich the sponges together with half of the cream, then smooth the rest over the top. Scatter over the coffee beans and dust with cocoa powder.

lemon drizzle loaf

Citrusy and sweet, this cake is a real teatime treat.

Serves 12
Preparation time 10 minutes
Cooking time 40 minutes

250 g (8 oz) butter, softened
250 g (8 oz) caster sugar
250 g (8 oz) brown rice flour
2 teaspoons gluten-free baking powder
4 eggs, beaten
grated rind and juice 1 lemon

for the lemon drizzle
grated rind and juice 2 lemons
100 g (3½ oz) caster sugar

Nutritional information:
Kcals 334 (1396 kj) Protein 5 g Carb 41 g
Fat 18 g Saturated fat 11 g Fibre 1 g

1 Grease and line a 900-g (2-lb) loaf tin. Place all the cake ingredients in a food processor and whiz until smooth, or beat in a large bowl.

2 Pour the mixture into the prepared tin and place in a preheated oven, 180°C (350°F) Gas Mark 4, for 35–40 minutes until golden and firm to the touch. Remove the cake from the oven and transfer to a wire rack.

3 Prick holes all over the sponge with a cocktail stick. Place the drizzle ingredients in a bowl and mix together, then drizzle the liquid over the warm loaf. Leave until completely cold. Decorate with a twist of lemon rind if desired.

beetroot speckle cake

This moist and beautifully coloured cake will make a big impression at afternoon tea.

Serves 10
Preparation time 15 minutes
Cooking time 50 minutes

200 g (7 oz) butter, melted
200 g (7 oz) light soft brown sugar
200 g (7 oz) raw beetroot, peeled and grated
150 g (5 oz) whole mixed nuts, toasted and chopped
3 eggs, separated
1 teaspoon gluten-free baking powder
½ teaspoon ground cinnamon
grated rind and juice 1 orange
200 g (7 oz) rice flour
3 tablespoons ground almonds

for the decoration
200 g (7 oz) cream cheese
1 tablespoon icing sugar
150 g (5 oz) whole mixed nuts

Nutritional information:
Kcals 595 (2487 kj) Protein 12 g Carb 38 g
Fat 44 g Saturated fat 19 g Fibre 4 g

SHOWN ON PAGES 38–39

1 Grease a 20-cm (8-inch) round deep cake tin. Place the butter and sugar in a large bowl and whisk together until pale. Stir in the beetroot, two thirds of the nuts and the egg yolks.

2 In another bowl, stir together the baking powder, cinnamon, orange rind and juice, rice flour and ground almonds. Add to the beetroot mixture and beat until smooth. In a separate clean bowl, whisk the egg whites until they form soft peaks, then fold them into the beetroot mixture.

3 Spoon the mixture into the prepared tin and place in a preheated oven, 200°C (400°F) Gas Mark 6, for 45–50 minutes. Remove the cake from the oven and transfer to a wire rack to cool.

4 Place the cream cheese and icing sugar in a bowl and beat together, then smooth the icing over the top of the cake. Decorate with the whole nuts.

banana and date bread

This is a real favourite with both young and old.
Spread with a little butter for a teatime treat.

Serves 12
Preparation time 20 minutes
Cooking time 1 hour

125 g (4 oz) stoned dates, roughly chopped
1 teaspoon bicarbonate of soda
2 tablespoons boiling water
100 g (3½ oz) butter, softened
100 g (3½ oz) caster sugar
2 eggs, beaten
3 large bananas, mashed
200 g (7 oz) rice flour
50 g (2 oz) cornflour
1 teaspoon gluten-free baking powder

Nutritional information:
Kcals 215 (899 kj) Protein 4 g Carb 33 g
Fat 8 g Saturated fat 2 g Fibre 2 g

1 Grease and line a 900-g (2-lb) loaf tin. Place the dates and bicarbonate of soda in a small bowl and pour over the water. Set aside for 10 minutes.

2 Meanwhile, place the butter and sugar in a large bowl and beat together until light and fluffy. Stir in the remaining ingredients, including the date mixture, and combine well.

3 Spoon the mixture into the prepared tin and place in a preheated oven, 180°C (350°F) Gas Mark 4, for about 1 hour until nicely browned and firm to the touch. Remove the loaf from the oven and transfer to a wire rack to cool. If you like, you could add a handful of roughly chopped mixed nuts to the mixture.

tropical fruit cake

The tropical fruit mix provides a good alternative to Christmas cake and has a lighter flavour.

Serves 14
Preparation time 15 minutes, plus
  soaking overnight
Cooking time 1½–2 hours

grated rind and juice 2 oranges
grated rind 1 lemon
300 g (10 oz) raisins
500 g (1 lb) dried tropical fruit, chopped
1 tablespoon crystallized ginger, chopped
3 tablespoons brandy
250 g (8 oz) butter, softened
250 g (8 oz) soft light brown sugar
100 g (3½ oz) soy flour
125 g (4 oz) rice flour
1 teaspoon ground mixed spice
75 g (3 oz) ground almonds
4 eggs, beaten

To decorate
300 g (10 oz) dried fruit or nuts
2 tablespoons apricot jam

Nutritional information:
Kcals 436 (1822 kj) **Protein** 7 g **Carb** 65 g
Fat 18 g **Saturated fat** 10 g **Fibre** 3 g

1 Place the orange rind and juice, lemon rind, raisins, dried fruit (we used papaya, peach, cranberries, apricots and pineapple), ginger and brandy in a non-metallic bowl, stir and cover, then leave overnight for the fruit to absorb the liquid.

2 Grease and line an 18 cm (7 inch) square deep cake tin (or a 20-cm/8-inch round tin) and tie a double thickness of brown paper or newspaper around the outside.

3 Place the butter and sugar in a bowl and beat together until light and fluffy. In another bowl, sift the flours and spice and stir in the ground almonds. Gradually add the beaten eggs to the creamed butter, adding a little flour mixture if it begins to curdle. Fold in the remaining flour mixture and the soaked fruit and any juice, then spoon into the prepared tin.

4 Place in a preheated oven, 170°C (325°F) Gas Mark 3, for 1½–2 hours or until a skewer inserted in the middle of the cake comes out clean. Remove the cake from the oven and transfer to a wire rack to cool. Decorate with dried fruit or nuts and glaze with sieved and warmed apricot jam.

carrot cake with passion-fruit topping

Moist and flavoursome, you can't beat a piece of carrot cake with a cup of tea!

Serves 12
Preparation time 10 minutes
Cooking time 40 minutes

375 g (12 oz) rice flour
1 tablespoon gluten-free baking powder
1 teaspoon mixed spice
250 g (8 oz) soft light brown sugar
300 g (10 oz) carrots, peeled and grated
200 g (7 oz) walnuts, chopped
100 ml (3½ fl oz) olive oil or
   rapeseed oil
4 tablespoons crème fraîche
3 eggs

for the topping
200 g (7 oz) cream cheese
2 tablespoons icing sugar
2 passion-fruit, flesh removed

Nutritional information:
Kcals 467 (1952 kj) Protein 9 g Carb 43 g
Fat 30 g Saturated fat 8 g Fibre 3 g

1 Grease and line a 20-cm (8-inch) loose-bottomed deep cake tin. Sift the flour, baking powder and spice together into a large bowl. Stir in the sugar, carrots and walnuts.

2 Place the oil, crème fraîche and eggs in another bowl and beat together, then stir into the dry ingredients. Spoon the mixture into the tin and place in a preheated oven, 180°C (350°F) Gas Mark 4, for 35–40 minutes, until a skewer inserted in the middle comes out clean. Remove the cake from the oven and transfer to a wire rack to cool.

3 To make the topping, place the cream cheese, icing sugar and passion-fruit flesh in a bowl and beat together. Smooth over the cake.

pistachio and citrus sand cake

A sandy-textured cake with a delicious fresh flavour and aroma.

Serves 14
Preparation time 10 minutes
Cooking time 50 minutes

200 g (7 oz) butter, softened
75 g (3 oz) golden caster sugar
3 eggs, beaten
175 g (6 oz) maize/cornflour
75 g (3 oz) ground almonds
1 teaspoon gluten-free baking powder
grated rind 1 orange
100 g (3½ oz) unsalted, shelled
  pistachios, roughly chopped

for the syrup topping
125 g (4 oz) caster sugar
grated rind and juice 1 lemon
grated rind and juice 1 orange

Nutritional information:
Kcals 281 (1175kj) Protein 4 g Carb 27 g
Fat 18 g Saturated fat 9 g Fibre 1 g

1 Grease a 23-cm (9-inch) ring mould and dust lightly with a little maize/cornflour. Place the butter and sugar in a large bowl and beat together. Add a little of the beaten eggs and the cornflour alternately, beating well, then stir in the remaining ingredients.

2 Spoon the mixture into the prepared tin and place in a preheated oven, 180°C (350°F) Gas Mark 4, for about 50 minutes until golden and a skewer inserted in the middle comes out clean. Remove the cake from the oven and transfer to a wire rack to cool.

3 Place the syrup ingredients in a saucepan, warm through until the sugar has dissolved, then boil for 2 minutes. Cool a little, then pour over the cake. Serve in wedges with a little creme fraiche.

hazelnut meringue stack

Light and airy meringue with a chewy centre – an unbeatable pud for a special occasion.

Serves 8
Preparation time 10 minutes
Cooking time 45 minutes, plus cooling

4 egg whites
250 g (8 oz) caster sugar
1 teaspoon white wine vinegar
100 g (3½ oz) hazelnuts, toasted and roughly chopped
200 ml (7 fl oz) whipping cream
275 g (9 oz) raspberries
a little cocoa powder for dusting

Nutritional information:
Kcals 298 (1246 kj) Protein 4 g Carb 32 g
Fat 18 g Saturated fat 7 g Fibre 2 g

1 Line three baking sheets with greaseproof paper. Place the egg whites in a large clean bowl and whisk until they form stiff peaks. Add half the sugar and continue to whisk until thick and glossy, then add the remaining sugar and the vinegar and whisk for 15 seconds.

2 Fold half of the hazelnuts into the mixture, then divide it between the three prepared trays, spooning the meringue into rounds roughly 18 cm (7 inches) in diameter. Place in a preheated oven, 150°C (300°F) Gas Mark 2, for 45 minutes then switch off the oven and leave the meringue to cool in the oven.

3 Whisk the cream until it forms soft peaks, spoon the cream over two of the meringues and top with the raspberries and remaining nuts, keeping back a few raspberries for decoration. Stack the meringues with the plain one on top, then dust with a little cocoa powder and decorate with the remaining raspberries. Eat on the same day or chill for up to 2 days.

blackberry and almond cake

This light sponge has a rather decadent mascarpone cream filling which complements it perfectly.

Serves 10
Preparation time 10 minutes
Cooking time 40 minutes

225 g (7½ oz) almonds
6 eggs, separated
200 g (7 oz) icing sugar, sifted
75 g (3 oz) gluten-free breadcrumbs
75 g (3 oz) butter, melted
300 g (10 oz) blackberries, roughly
   crushed

for the filling
250 g (8 oz) mascarpone cheese
2 tablespoons icing sugar
few drops vanilla essence

Nutritional information:
Kcals 371 (1551 kj) Protein 7 g Carb 22 g
Fat 28 g Saturated fat 13 g Fibre 3 g

1 Grease and line a 23-cm (9-inch) deep spring-form tin. Place the almonds on a baking sheet and place in a preheated oven, 180°C (350°F) Gas Mark 4, for 10 minutes until golden. Allow to cool a little, then place in a food processor or liquidizer and whiz until they resemble fine breadcrumbs.

2 Place the egg whites in a large clean bowl and whisk until they form soft peaks. Add 2 tablespoons of the icing sugar and whisk until firm. Place the egg yolks in a separate bowl with the remaining icing sugar and whisk until pale. Fold in the breadcrumbs, butter, half the blackberries and the egg whites, then transfer to the prepared tin. Place in the oven for 40 minutes, then transfer to a wire rack to cool.

3 Place the filling ingredients in a bowl and beat together, along with the the remaining blackberries. Slice the cake in half and fill with the mascarpone mixture.

cherry and ricotta cake

Adding ricotta keeps this cake lovely and moist, and the flavours and textures blend beautifully.

Serves 12
Preparation time 10 minutes
Cooking time 1½ hours

200 g (7 oz) polenta
200 g (7 oz) brown rice flour
1 teaspoon gluten-free baking powder
few drops almond essence
250 g (8 oz) caster sugar
250 g (8 oz) ricotta cheese
100 g (3½ oz) butter, melted
300 g (10 oz) can black cherries in juice

for the topping:
25 g (1 oz) demerara sugar
50 g (2 oz) blanched almonds, cut into
   slivers

Nutritional information:
Kcals 393 (1643 kj) **Protein** 6 g **Carb** 58 g
Fat 16 g **Saturated fat** 9 g **Fibre** 3 g

1 Grease and lightly flour a 20-cm (8-inch) spring-form cake tin. Sift the polenta, flour and baking powder together into a large bowl, then beat in the almond essence, sugar, ricotta, butter and cherries with their juice.

2 Spoon the mixture into the prepared tin, mix together the topping ingredients and sprinkle over the top of the cake. Place the cake in a preheated oven, 170°C (325°F) Gas Mark 3, for 1½ hours until golden and a skewer inserted in the middle comes out clean. Remove the cake from the oven and transfer to a wire rack to cool.

tempting tray bakes and biscuits

coconut macaroons

Light but with a chewy texture, these classic macaroons make a tempting afternoon nibble.

Makes 14 macaroons
Preparation time 10 minutes
Cooking time 20 minutes

3 egg whites
150 g (5 oz) golden caster sugar
2 tablespoons ground almonds
250 g (8 oz) desiccated coconut

Nutritional information:
Kcals 165 (690 kj) Protein 2 g Carb 12 g
Fat 12 g Saturated fat 9 g Fibre 3 g

1 Line two baking sheets with nonstick baking paper, or you could use edible rice paper. Place the egg whites in a large clean bowl and whisk until they form stiff peaks. Gradually whisk in the sugar until thick and glossy, then fold in the almonds and coconut.

2 Place seven spoonfuls of mixture on each tray and place in a preheated oven, 180°C (350°F) Gas Mark 4, for 15–20 minutes until turning golden. Remove from the oven and transfer to a wire rack to cool.

lemon madeleines

These light lemony bites make a delicate addition
to afternoon tea.

Makes 36 cakes
Preparation time 10 minutes, plus
resting time of 30 minutes
Cooking time 8 minutes

2 large eggs
4 tablespoons caster sugar
100 g (3½ oz) white rice flour
100 g (3½ oz) butter, melted, plus extra
for greasing
grated rind 1 lemon
icing sugar to dust

Nutritional information:
Kcals 44 (184 kj) Protein 1 g Carb 4 g
Fat 2 g Saturated fat 1 g Fibre 0 g

1 Place the eggs and sugar in a large bowl and whisk together until pale and thick. Sift the flour into the mixture and fold it in. Drizzle in the melted butter, add the lemon rind and stir to combine. Set the mixture aside for half an hour.

2 Generously grease 36 holes in three 12-hole madeleine or mini muffin tins with plenty of butter. Spoon about 1 teaspoon of mixture into each mould and place in a preheated oven, 220°C (425°F) Gas Mark 7, for about 8 minutes until just firm.

3 Remove the madeleines from the oven and transter to a wire rack to cool, then dust generously with icing sugar. They are best eaten on the same day.

chocolate caramel shortbread

A real favourite: creamy caramel on light, crisp shortbread topped with thick swirls of chocolate.

Makes 15 pieces
Preparation time 20 minutes, plus chilling
Cooking time 15 minutes

100 g (3½ oz) butter, softened
50 g (2 oz) caster sugar
100 g (3½ oz) brown rice flour
100 g (3½ oz) maize/cornflour

for the caramel
100 g (3½ oz) butter
50 g (2 oz) soft light brown sugar
397 g (13 oz) can condensed milk

for the topping
100 g (3½ oz) gluten-free white chocolate
100 g (3½ oz) gluten-free plain chocolate

Nutritional information:
Kcals 328 (1371 kj) **Protein** 4 g **Carb** 40 g
Fat 17 g **Saturated fat** 11 g **Fibre** 0 g

1 Place the butter and sugar in a large bowl and beat together until light and fluffy, then stir in the flours until well combined. Press the shortbread into a 28 x 18-cm (11 x 7-inch) baking tin, then place in a preheated oven, 200°C (400°F) Gas Mark 6, for 10–12 minutes until golden.

2 Meanwhile, place the caramel ingredients in a heavy-based saucepan and heat over a low heat until the sugar has dissolved, then cook for 5 minutes, stirring continuously. Remove from the heat and leave to cool a little, then pour the caramel over the shortbread base and leave to cool.

3 Place the white and dark chocolate in separate heatproof bowls over pans of simmering water and leave until melted. When the caramel is firm, spoon alternate spoonfuls of the white and plain chocolate over the caramel, tap the tin on the work surface so that the different chocolates join, then use a knife to make swirls in the chocolate. Refrigerate until set, then cut into 15 squares.

fruity shortbread fingers

Full of flavour and texture, these are a hit with children and make a filling yet healthy addition to lunch boxes.

Makes 12 bars
Preparation time 10 minutes
Cooking time 25 minutes

100 g (3½ oz) butter, softened
50 g (2 oz) caster sugar
100 g (3½ oz) brown rice flour
100 g (3½ oz) maize/cornflour
150 g (5 oz) ready-to-eat dried dates,
   roughly chopped
grated rind and juice 1 orange

for the topping
100 g (3½ oz) runny honey
50 g (2 oz) butter, melted
40 g (1½ oz) gluten-free cornflakes,
   roughly crushed
2 tablespoons desiccated coconut
75 g (3 oz) ready-to-eat dried apricots,
   chopped
2 tablespoons mixed seeds, e.g.
   pumpkin and sunflower

Nutritional information:
Kcals 272 (1137 kj) Protein 2 g Carb 40 g
Fat 13 g Saturated fat 8 g Fibre 0 g

1 Place the butter and sugar in a large bowl and beat together until light and fluffy, then stir in the flours until well combined. Press the shortbread into a 28 x 18-cm (11 x 7-inch) baking tin and place in a preheated oven, 200°C (400°F) Gas Mark 6, for 10 minutes.

2 Meanwhile, place the dates and orange rind and juice in a small saucepan, bring to the boil and simmer gently until pulpy. Remove from the heat and leave to cool a little, then spread the mixture over the shortbread base.

3 Place all the topping ingredients in a bowl and mix together, spoon the mixture over the dates and press down gently. Place in the oven for 12–15 minutes until golden. Remove from the oven, leave to cool a little, then cut into 12 bars and cool completely before removing from the tin.

espresso and white chocolate brownies

These squidgy white chocolate brownies are given a twist with the addition of some espresso.

Makes 15 brownies
Preparation time 10 minutes
Cooking time 30 minutes

75 g (3 oz) gluten-free white chocolate
75 g (3 oz) butter
175 g (6 oz) soft light brown sugar
2 eggs, beaten
few drops vanilla extract
50 g (2 oz) ground almonds
100 g (3½ oz) rice flour
2 teaspoons instant espresso, dissolved
   in 1 tablespoon water
100 g (3½ oz) walnuts toasted and
   roughly chopped

Nutritional information:
Kcals 210 (878 kj) Protein 3 g Carb 22 g
Fat 13 g Saturated fat 2 g Fibre 0 g

1 Grease and line a 28 x 18-cm (11 x 7-inch) baking tin. Place the chocolate and butter in a large heatproof bowl over a pan of simmering water and leave until melted. Stir all the remaining ingredients in roughly, then pour into the prepared tin.

2 Place in a preheated oven, 180°C (350°F) Gas Mark 4, for 30 minutes until slightly springy in the centre. Remove from the oven and leave to cool for 10 minutes before marking into 15 squares, then cool on a wire rack.

chewy nutty chocolate brownies

These spectacular gooey squares are great for a treat with coffee or served as a dessert with a little cream or gluten-free ice cream.

Makes 15 pieces
Preparation time 10 minutes
Cooking time 30 minutes

75 g (3 oz) gluten-free plain chocolate
100 g (3½ oz) butter
200 g (7 oz) soft light brown sugar
2 eggs, beaten
few drops vanilla extract
50 g (2 oz) ground almonds
25 g (1 oz) brown rice flour
150 g (5 oz) mixed nuts, toasted and
   roughly chopped

Nutritional information:
Kcals 230 (961 kj) Protein 3 g Carb 19 g
Fat 16 g Saturated fat 5 g Fibre 1 g

1 Grease and line a 28 x 18-cm (11 x 7-inch) baking tin. Place the chocolate and butter in a large heatproof bowl over a pan of simmering water and leave until melted. Stir in all the remaining ingredients and combine well.

2 Pour the mixture into the prepared tin and place in a preheated oven, 180°C (350°F) Gas Mark 4, for 30 minutes until slightly springy in the centre. Remove from the oven and cool for 10 minutes in the tin, then mark into 15 squares.

hazelnut and chocolate macaroons

These flavoursome macaroons are quite different to the traditional coconut version, but no less moreish.

Makes 12 macaroons
Preparation time 10 minutes
Cooking time 20 minutes

3 egg whites
150 g (5 oz) caster sugar
150 g (5 oz) hazelnuts, toasted and
  ground
2 tablespoons cocoa powder
few drops vanilla extract
100 g (3½ oz) gluten-free milk chocolate

Nutritional information:
Kcals 148 (619 kj) Protein 4 g Carb 11 g
Fat 10 g Saturated fat 1 g Fibre 2 g

1 Line two baking sheets with nonstick baking paper, or you could use edible rice paper. Place the egg whites in a large clean bowl and whisk until they form stiff peaks. Gradually whisk in the sugar until thick and glossy, then fold in the hazelnuts, cocoa powder and vanilla extract.

2 Place six spoonfuls of mixture on each tray and place in a preheated oven, 180°C (350°F) Gas Mark 4, for 15–20 minutes. Remove from the oven and transfer to a wire rack to cool.

3 Place the chocolate in a heatproof bowl over a pan of simmering water and leave until melted, then drizzle it over the macaroons.

plum pastries

These are good as a dessert for summer entertaining
when plums are juicy, ripe and plentiful.

Makes 6 pastries
Preparation time 15 minutes, plus
  chilling
Cooking time 25 minutes

75 g (3 oz) brown rice flour
75 g (3 oz) polenta
½ teaspoon xanthan gum
good pinch mixed spice
grated rind ½ lemon
100 g (3½ oz) butter, cubed
1 tablespoon golden caster sugar
1 egg yolk, beaten
100 g (3½ oz) marzipan, grated
3 tablespoons crème fraîche
500 g (1 lb) plums, halved and stoned
2 tablespoons apricot jam, warmed

Nutritional information:
Kcals 247 (1032 kj) Protein 3 g Carb 38 g
Fat 10 g Saturated fat 5 g Fibre 1 g

1 Place the flour, polenta, xanthan gum, mixed spice, lemon rind, butter and sugar in a food processor and whiz until the mixture resembles fine breadcrumbs, or rub in by hand in a large bowl.

2 Very gently add the egg yolk and mix in using a knife, adding a little cold water if the mixture is too dry. Knead the mixture into a ball, wrap closely and chill for 30 minutes.

3 Divide the pastry into six, then roll each piece out on a surface dusted lightly with rice flour to a rectangle approximately 10 x 6 cm (4 x 2½ inches) and mark a border about 1 cm (½ inch) from the edge of the pastry.

4 Place the pastry on a baking sheet. Mix together the marzipan and crème fraîche and spoon over the pastry within the border; arrange the plums over the marzipan mixture and place in a preheated oven, 200°C (400°F) Gas Mark 6, for 20–25 minutes until the pastry is golden and the plums are beginning to ooze a little juice. Remove the pastries from the oven and leave to cool. Brush each with a little jam. Delicious served with cream or crème fraîche for pudding.

bakewell slice

This gluten-free version of a traditional family cake tastes just as good as the original.

Makes 12 pieces
Preparation time 20 minutes
Cooking time 25 minutes

75 g (3 oz) polenta
75 g (3 oz) brown rice flour
½ teaspoon xanthan gum
grated rind 1 lemon
100 g (3½ oz) butter, cubed
1 tablespoon golden caster sugar
1 egg yolk, beaten
4 tablespoons raspberry jam

for the sponge
2 eggs
125 g (4 oz) caster sugar
125 g (4 oz) rice flour
125 g (4 oz) butter
50 g (2 oz) ground almonds
1 teaspoon gluten-free baking powder
50 g (2 oz) flaked almonds

Nutritional information:
Kcals 301 (1258 kj) Protein 5 g Carb 30 g
Fat 18 g Saturated fat 9 g Fibre 1 g

1 Place the polenta, flour, xanthan gum, lemon rind, butter and sugar in a food processor and whiz until the mixture resembles fine breadcrumbs, or rub in by hand in a large bowl. Add the egg yolk and gently mix in using a knife, adding a little cold water if the mixture is too dry.

2 Place the pastry in an 28 x 18-cm (11 x 7-inch) deep baking tin and press it out to line the tin. Spread the jam over the pastry.

3 Place all the sponge ingredients except the flaked almonds in a food processor and whiz until smooth, or beat in a large bowl. Spoon the mixture into the baking tray, and place in a preheated oven, 200°C (400°F) Gas Mark 6, for 20–25 minutes until just firm and risen. Remove the tart from the oven and leave to cool. Toast the flaked almonds for a few minutes under a grill until brown and scatter them over the top. Cut into 12 pieces.

pistachio and choc chip shortbread

This light, melt-in-the-mouth shortbread has the ever-popular flavour of chocolate in it as well as the more unusual addition of pistachios.

Makes 12 pieces
Preparation time 10 minutes
Cooking time 20 minutes

100 g (3½ oz) butter, softened
50 g (2 oz) caster sugar
100 g (3½ oz) rice flour
100 g (3½ oz) maize/cornflour
50 g (2 oz) gluten-free plain chocolate
  drops or gluten-free plain chocolate,
  chopped
50 g (2 oz) pistachios, chopped

for the decoration
75 g (3 oz) gluten-free plain
  chocolate, melted

Nutritional information:
Kcals 175 (732 kj) Protein 1 g Carb 22 g
Fat 10 g Saturated fat 2 g Fibre 0 g

SHOWN ON PAGES 66–67

1 Place the butter and sugar in a large bowl and beat together until light and fluffy. Stir in the remaining ingredients until well combined. Press the mixture into a 28 x 18-cm (11 x 7-inch) baking tin and place in a preheated oven, 180°C (350°F) Gas Mark 4, for 20 minutes until golden.

2 Remove the shortbread from the oven, mark into 12 triangles then place on a wire rack to cool completely before removing from the tin. It is sometimes easier to remove the shortbread from the tin once it has been chilled a little. Drizzle with the melted chocolate.

peanutty squares

These are simple to make but should be served in small pieces, as the combination of peanut butter and chocolate makes them very rich.

Makes 24 pieces
Preparation time 10 minutes
Cooking time 25 minutes

50 g (2 oz) butter, softened
200 g (7 oz) icing sugar
175 g (6 oz) gluten-free crunchy peanut
  butter
100 g (3½ oz) brown rice flour
1 egg, beaten
200 g (7 oz) gluten-free plain chocolate
1 tablespoon butter

Nutritional information:
Kcals 156 (652 kj) Protein 3 g Carb 17 g
Fat 9 g Saturated fat 4 g Fibre 1 g

1 Grease and line a 23-cm (9-inch) square baking tin. Place the butter and sugar in a large bowl, beat together until pale and fluffy, then stir in the peanut butter, flour and egg.

2 Spoon the mixture into the prepared tin and place in a preheated oven, 200°C (400°F) Gas Mark 6, for 20–25 minutes. Remove the tin from the oven and leave to cool.

3 Place the chocolate and butter in a heatproof bowl over a pan of simmering water and leave until the chocolate is melted, then pour over the biscuit mixture. Leave to cool until the chocolate is set, then mark into 24 small squares.

lemon, pistachio and fruit squares

Chewy and with so many great flavours, these are great for a high-energy snack.

Makes 15–20 pieces
Preparation time 10 minutes
Cooking time 20 minutes

grated rind 1 lemon
75 g (3 oz) ready-to-eat dried dates, chopped
75 g (3 oz) unsalted pistachios, chopped
75 g (3 oz) flaked almonds, chopped
125 g (4 oz) soft light brown sugar
150 g (5 oz) millet flakes
40 g (1½ oz) gluten-free cornflakes, lightly crushed
397 g (13 oz) tin condensed milk
25 g (1 oz) mixed seeds, e.g. pumpkin and sunflower

Nutritional information:
Kcals 174 (728 kj) Protein 4 g Carb 26 g
Fat 6 g Saturated fat 2 g Fibre 2 g

1 Simply place all the ingredients in a large bowl and mix together. Spoon into a 28 x 18-cm (11 x 7-inch) baking tin and place in a preheated oven, 180°C (350°F) Gas Mark 4, for 20 minutes.

2 Remove from the oven, leave to cool, then mark into 15–20 squares and chill until firm. If you fancy, you could drizzle the top with some melted chocolate once the squares are cooled.

lemony poppets

These lemon and ground almond creations are so
light, one won't be enough!

Makes 30 poppets
Preparation time 10 minutes, plus
  chilling
Cooking time 20 minutes

100 g (3½ oz) white vegetable fat
100 g (3½ oz) butter, softened
100 g (3½ oz) caster sugar
1 egg yolk
grated rind 1 lemon
1 tablespoon milk
200 g (7 oz) brown rice flour
2 tablespoons maize/cornflour
50 g (2 oz) ground almonds

Nutritional information:
Kcals 98 (410 kj) Protein 0 g Carb 10 g
Fat 6 g Saturated fat 4 g Fibre 0 g

1 Line two baking sheets with nonstick baking paper. Place all the
ingredients in a food processor and whiz until smooth, or beat in
a large bowl until light and smooth.

2 Spoon the mixture on to a surface dusted lightly with rice flour,
divide it into 30 and roll into balls. Place on the prepared baking
sheets, flatten slightly with your thumb and chill for 30 minutes.
Place in a preheated oven, 180°C (350°F) Gas Mark 4, for about
20 minutes until golden. Remove from the oven and leave to cool
on the baking sheets.

walnut biscuits

These are very easy to make, and you could use other flavours, such as raisin or choc chip, to suit your taste.

Makes 30 biscuits
Preparation time 10 minutes
Cooking time 20 minutes

125 g (4 oz) butter, softened
125 g (4 oz) golden caster sugar
1 egg yolk
125 g (4 oz) rice flour
1 teaspoon gluten-free baking powder
100 g (3½ oz) walnuts, chopped

Nutritional information:
Kcals 86 (359 kj) Protein 1 g Carb 8 g
Fat 6 g Saturated fat 2 g Fibre 0 g

1 Place the butter and sugar in a large bowl and beat together until light and fluffy. Beat in the egg yolk, followed by the remaining ingredients to give a smooth soft dough.

2 Place walnut-sized pieces of the mixture on to baking sheets and place in a preheated oven, 180°C (350°F) Gas Mark 4, for 15–20 minutes until golden. Remove the biscuits from the oven, leave for a few minutes to harden, then transfer to a wire rack to cool.

chocolate chip cookies

This gluten-free version of these perennial favourites
is light, crunchy and simply irresistible.

Makes 30 cookies
Preparation time 10 minutes
Cooking time 10 minutes

75 g (3 oz) butter, softened
100 g (3½ oz) caster sugar
75 g (3 oz) soft light brown sugar
1 egg, beaten
150 g (5 oz) brown rice flour
½ teaspoon bicarbonate of soda
1 tablespoon cocoa powder
75 g (3 oz) gluten-free plain chocolate
  chips

Nutritional information:
Kcals 75 (314 kj) Protein 0 g Carb 12 g
Fat 3 g Saturated fat 2 g Fibre 0 g

1 Place all the ingredients except the chocolate chips in a food processor and whiz until smooth, or beat in a large bowl. Stir in the chocolate chips, and bring the mixture together with your hands to form a ball.

2 On a surface dusted lightly with rice flour, divide the mixture into 30 balls, then place them on baking sheets, well spaced apart, pressing down gently with the back of a fork.

3 Place in a preheated oven, 180°C (350°F) Gas Mark 4, for 8–10 minutes. Remove the cookies from the oven, leave for a few minutes to harden, then transfer to a wire rack to cool.

apricot almond crunch biscuits

These little flapjacky morsels are great
for a teatime treat.

Makes 15 biscuits
Preparation time 10 minutes
Cooking time 15 minutes

100 g (3½ oz) butter
50 g (2 oz) demerara sugar
1 tablespoon golden syrup
100 g (3½ oz) brown rice flour
½ teaspoon gluten-free baking powder
100 g (3½ oz) millet flakes
75 g (3 oz) ready-to-eat dried apricots,
   chopped
50 g (2 oz) blanched almonds, toasted
   and roughly chopped

Nutritional information:
Kcals 137 (573 kj) Protein 2 g Carb 15 g
Fat 8 g Saturated fat 6 g Fibre 1 g

1 Place the butter, sugar and syrup in a large saucepan over a gentle heat and melt together. Stir in the remaining ingredients so that everything is well mixed.

2 Scrape the mixture out on to a surface lightly dusted with rice flour and use your hands to bring it together. Divide the mixture into 15 pieces, roll into balls, then place on two baking sheets and flatten to rounds about 5 cm (2 inches) in diameter.

3 Place in a preheated oven, 180°C (350°F) Gas Mark 4, for 15 minutes. Remove the biscuits from the oven, leave for a few minutes to harden, then transfer to a wire rack to cool.

crisp ginger biscuits

Not only deliciously crisp but also perfect for dunking in tea or coffee.

Makes 20 biscuits
Preparation time 10 minutes
Cooking time 15 minutes

200 g (7 oz) brown rice flour
50 g (2 oz) ground almonds
½ teaspoon ground ginger
100 g (3½ oz) caster sugar
1 piece preserved ginger, very finely
  chopped
1 egg, beaten
100 g (3½ oz) butter, melted

Nutritional information:
Kcals 111 (464 kj) Protein 1 g Carb 15 g
Fat 6 g Saturated fat 3 g Fibre 0 g

1 Place all the dry ingredients and the preserved ginger in a large bowl and stir together. Combine the egg and butter and stir into the flour mixture.

2 Scrape the mixture out on to a surface lightly dusted with rice flour and use your hands to bring it together. Divide the mixture into 20 pieces, roll into balls then place on two–three baking sheets, pressing down slightly.

3 Place in a preheated oven, 180°C (350°F) Gas Mark 4, for 12–15 minutes until golden. Remove the biscuits from the oven, leave for a few minutes to harden, then transfer to a wire rack to cool.

orange and polenta crispy cookies

Polenta gives these biscuits a really crisp and crunchy texture.

Makes 20 cookies
Preparation time 10 minutes, plus chilling
Cooking time 8 minutes

75 g (3 oz) polenta
25 g (1 oz) rice flour
25 g (1 oz) ground almonds
½ teaspoon gluten-free baking powder
75 g (3 oz) icing sugar
50 g (2 oz) butter, cubed
1 egg yolk, beaten
grated rind 1 orange
25 g (1 oz) flaked almonds

Nutritional information:
Kcals 67 (280 kj) Protein 1 g Carb 7 g
Fat 4 g Saturated fat 1 g Fibre 1 g

1 Cover two baking sheets with nonstick baking paper. Place the polenta, flour, ground almonds, baking powder, icing sugar and butter in a food processor and whiz until the mixture resembles fine breadcrumbs, or rub in by hand in a large bowl.

2 Stir in the egg yolk and orange rind and bring together to make a dough. Wrap closely and chill for 30 minutes.

3 Remove the dough from the refrigerator and roll out thinly on a surface dusted lightly with rice flour. Cut into 20 rounds with a 4-cm (1½-inch) cutter. Transfer to the prepared baking sheets, sprinkle with the almonds and place in a preheated oven, 180°C (350°F) Gas Mark 4, for about 8 minutes until golden. Remove the cookies from the oven, leave for a few minutes to harden, then transfer to a wire rack to cool.

something
savoury

white loaf

Use on the day of baking for bread or toast that
doesn't turn to crumbs!

Serves 12
Preparation time 20 minutes, plus
proving
Cooking time 1 hour

675 g (1 lb 6 oz) brown rice flour, plus
  a little extra for dusting
1 tablespoon xanthan gum
2 tablespoons skimmed dried milk
  powder
½ teaspoon salt
2 x 7 g (¼ oz) sachets fast-action dried
  yeast
2 teaspoons granulated sugar
450 ml (¾ pint) warm water
2 eggs, beaten
2 tablespoons olive oil

Nutritional information:
Kcals 208 (869 kj) Protein 8 g Carb 40 g
Fat 4 g Saturated fat 0 g Fibre 2 g

SHOWN ON PAGES 92–93

1 Place the flour, xanthan gum, skimmed milk powder and salt in
a large bowl and mix together. Place the yeast, sugar and water
in another bowl and stand it in a warm place for 10 minutes until
frothy. Pour the yeast mixture, eggs and oil into the dry ingredients
and stir together to form a soft dough. Tip the dough out on to a
surface dusted lightly with rice flour and knead for 5 minutes.

2 Place the dough in a lightly oiled bowl, cover with a damp tea
towel or clingfilm and leave to rise in a warm place for about
1 hour or until doubled in size. Tip the dough out and reknead then
form into a long, oval bloomer shape, place on a baking tray and
leave to rise again until it has doubled in size. Score along the top a
few times using a knife.

3 Place in a preheated oven, 200°C (400°F) Gas Mark 6, for
45–50 minutes or until golden and hollow-sounding when
tapped. Remove the loaf from the tray and return to the oven for
5–10 minutes to crisp it all over. Remove the loaf from the oven and
transfer to a wire rack to cool.

soda bread

This great free-form bread is super-quick and
easy to make.

Makes 8 pieces
Preparation time 10 minutes
Cooking time 35 minutes

200 g (7 oz) brown rice flour, plus extra
   for dusting
175 g (6 oz) maize/cornflour
25 g (1 oz) rice bran
2 tablespoons skimmed dried milk
   powder
½ teaspoon bicarbonate of soda
1 teaspoon gluten-free baking powder
good pinch salt
1 teaspoon xanthan gum
pinch caster sugar
1 egg, lightly beaten
300 ml (½ pint) buttermilk
4 tablespoons water

Nutritional information:
Kcals 175 (732 kj) Protein 8 g Carb 32 g
Fat 2 g Saturated fat 0 g Fibre 4 g

1 Place all the dry ingredients in a large bowl and mix together. Place the egg, buttermilk and water in another bowl, mix together, then stir into the dry ingredients.

2 Tip the mixture out on to a surface dusted lightly with rice flour and form into a round about 20 cm (8 inches) in diameter. Mark into eight segments, then place on a baking sheet and sprinkle over a little extra rice flour.

3 Place in an oven preheated to its highest setting and cook for 10 minutes, then reduce the heat to 200°C (400°F) Gas Mark 6 and continue to cook for about 25 minutes until golden and hollow-sounding when tapped. Remove the loaf from the oven and transfer to a wire rack to cool.

feta and herb loaf

This cheesy herb loaf makes a really nice change
from the usual gluten-free bread.

Serves 14
Preparation time 10 minutes, plus
  proving
Cooking time 45 minutes

200 g (7 oz) polenta
100 g (3½ oz) rice flour
50 g (2 oz) dried milk powder
pinch salt
7 g (¼ oz) sachet fast-action dried yeast
2 teaspoons caster sugar
2 teaspoons xanthan gum
3 eggs, beaten
2 tablespoons chopped fresh mixed
  herbs
450 ml (¾ pint) tepid water
100 g (3½ oz) feta cheese, crumbled

Nutritional information:
Kcals 118 (493 kj) Protein 6 g Carb 16 g
Fat 3 g Saturated fat 1 g Fibre 1 g

1 Grease and line a 900-g (2-lb) loaf tin. Sift the polenta, flour, milk powder and salt into a large bowl and stir well to combine. Stir in the yeast, sugar and xanthan gum.

2 Place the eggs, herbs and water in a bowl and mix together. Stir this mixture into the dry ingredients and combine to form a soft dough. Beat for 5 minutes, then stir in the feta.

3 Spoon the mixture into the prepared tin, cover with a clean damp tea towel and leave in a warm place to rise for about 30 minutes, until the mixture is near the top of the tin. Place in a preheated oven, 180°C (350°F) Gas Mark 4, for about 45 minutes until brown and hollow when tapped. Remove the loaf from the oven and transfer to a wire rack to cool.

pumpkin loaf

This simple loaf is delicious served with cheese and chutney, giving a new take on a ploughman's lunch.

Serves 12
Preparation time 10 minutes
Cooking time 1 hour

250 g (8 oz) brown rice flour
250 g (8 oz) maize/cornflour
pinch salt
½ teaspoon ground cinnamon
½ teaspoon grated nutmeg
2 teaspoons gluten-free baking powder
1 tablespoon xanthan gum
300 g (10 oz) cooked pumpkin, puréed
1 tablespoon runny honey
2 tablespoons olive oil
3 eggs, beaten
150 ml (¼ pint) water

Nutritional information:
Kcals 186 (778 kj) Protein 6 g Carb 30 g
Fat 4 g Saturated fat 0 g Fibre 3 g

1 Grease and line a 900-g (2-lb) loaf tin. Place all the dry ingredients in a large bowl and mix together. Place the remaining ingredients in another bowl, mix together, then stir into the dry ingredients and beat well.

2 Pour into the prepared tin and place in a preheated oven, 180°C (350°F) Gas Mark 4, for about 1 hour until golden, risen and firm to the touch. Remove the loaf from the oven and transfer to a wire rack to cool, then serve buttered.

corn bread

An American favourite, this is great served with soups and casseroles to mop up all the flavours.

Makes 9 pieces
Preparation time 10 minutes
Cooking time 20 minutes

250 g (8 oz) polenta
175 g (6 oz) chickpea/gram flour
2 teaspoons caster sugar
2 teaspoons gluten-free baking powder
pinch salt
3 spring onions, finely sliced
2 tablespoons olive oil
600 ml (1 pint) milk
1 egg

Nutritional information:
Kcals 104 (435 kj) Protein 5 g Carb 10 g
Fat 4 g Saturated fat 1g Fibre 2 g

1 Grease a 20-cm (8-inch) square nonstick baking tin. Place the polenta, flour, sugar, baking powder, salt and spring onions in a large bowl and mix together.

2 In a separate bowl, beat together the oil, milk and egg, then pour this mixture over the dry ingredients and stir well to combine. Transfer the dough to the prepared tin and place in a preheated oven, 200°C (400°F) Gas Mark 6, for 20 minutes until golden and firm Cut into nine pieces and leave to cool.

nutty seed loaf

The nuts and seeds give this loaf a really nice texture as well as plenty of flavour. It's great served toasted.

Makes 8 pieces
Preparation time 10 minutes
Cooking time 25 minutes

400 g (13 oz) brown rice flour, plus extra for dusting
25 g (1 oz) rice bran
2 tablespoons skimmed dried milk powder
½ teaspoon bicarbonate of soda
1 teaspoon gluten-free baking powder
½–1 teaspoon salt
1 teaspoon xanthan gum
pinch caster sugar
50 g (2 oz) mixed seeds, e.g. sunflower and pumpkin
50 g (2 oz) hazelnuts, toasted and roughly chopped
1 egg, lightly beaten
300 ml (½ pint) buttermilk

Nutritional information:
Kcals 263 (1099 kj) Protein 10 g Carb 37 g
Fat 8 g Saturated fat 1 g Fibre 4 g

1 Place all the dry ingredients, including the nuts, in a large bowl and mix together. In a separate bowl, mix together the egg and buttermilk, then stir into the dry ingredients.

2 Tip the dough out on to a surface dusted lightly with rice flour and form into a round about 20 cm (8 inches) in diameter. Mark into eight segments, then place on a baking sheet and dust with a little extra rice flour.

3 Place in an oven preheated to its highest setting and cook for 10 minutes, then reduce the heat to 200°C (400°F) Gas Mark 6 and continue to cook for about 15 minutes until the loaf is golden and sounds hollow when tapped. Remove the loaf from the oven and transfer to a wire rack to cool.

walnut loaf

Buckwheat gives this delicious bread an 'earthy'
nutty taste with a wonderful aroma.

Serves 12
Preparation time 25 minutes, plus
  proving
Cooking time 1 hour

250 g (8 oz) buckwheat flour
500 g (1 lb) brown rice flour, plus a little
  extra for dusting
1 tablespoon xanthan gum
2 tablespoons skimmed dried milk
  powder
200 g (7 oz) walnut pieces
½ teaspoon salt
2 x 7 g (¼ oz) sachets fast-action dried
  yeast
2 teaspoons caster sugar
450 ml (¾ pint) warm water
2 eggs, beaten
2 tablespoons runny honey
2 tablespoons olive oil

Nutritional information:
Kcals 360 (1505 kj) Protein 8 g Carb 46 g
Fat 16 g Saturated fat 1 g Fibre 1 g

1 Grease a 900-g (2-lb) loaf tin. Place the flours, xanthan gum, milk powder, walnut pieces and salt in a large bowl. Place the yeast, sugar and water in another bowl and stand it in a warm place for 10 minutes until frothy. Pour the yeast mixture, eggs, honey and oil into the flour mixture and stir together to form a soft dough. Tip the dough out on to a surface dusted lightly with rice flour and knead for 5 minutes.

2 Place the dough in a lightly oiled bowl, cover with a damp cloth or cling film and leave to rise in a warm place for about 1 hour or until doubled in size. Tip the dough out and reknead, then place in the prepared loaf tin and leave to rise again.

3 Place in a preheated oven, 200°C (400°F) Gas Mark 6, for 45–50 minutes or until golden and hollow-sounding when tapped. Remove the loaf from the tin and return to the oven for 5–10 minutes to crisp it all over. Remove the loaf from the oven and transfer to a wire rack to cool.

buckwheat bread

This is fantastic served warm with butter and jam
for afternoon tea.

Serves 8
Preparation time 10 minutes, plus
  proving
Cooking time 50 minutes

200 g (7 oz) buckwheat flour
200 g (7 oz) brown rice flour
2 teaspoons xanthan gum
2 tablespoons dried milk powder
7 g (¼ oz) sachet fast-action dried yeast
2 teaspoons caster sugar
300 ml (½ pint) warm water
2 eggs, beaten

for the glaze
1 egg, beaten
1 tablespoon milk

Nutritional information:
Kcals 220 (920 kj) Protein 7 g Carb 43 g
Fat 3 g Saturated fat 1 g Fibre 4 g

1 Place the flours, xanthan gum and dried milk powder in a large
bowl and mix together. Place the yeast, sugar and water in
another bowl and stand it in a warm place for 15 minutes until
frothy. Pour the yeast mixture into the dry ingredients with the
beaten eggs and bring together to form a soft dough.

2 Tip the dough out on to a surface dusted lightly with rice flour and
knead for 5 minutes. Shape the dough into a loaf, place on a baking
sheet and cover with a damp cloth. Leave to rise for 40 minutes.

3 Place the egg and milk for the glaze in a bowl, mix together, then
brush over the loaf. Place the loaf in a preheated oven, 200°C
(400°F) Gas Mark 6, for 45–50 minutes, until golden and hollow-
sounding when tapped. Remove the loaf from the oven and transfer
to a wire rack to cool.

parmesan, olive and sun-dried tomato loaf

There is a taste of the Mediterranean in this simple loaf.

Serves 14
Preparation time 10 minutes, plus proving
Cooking time 45 minutes

200 g (7 oz) polenta
100 g (3½ oz) rice flour
50 g (2 oz) dried milk powder
pinch salt
7 g (¼ oz) sachet fast-action dried yeast
2 teaspoons caster sugar
2 teaspoons xanthan gum
3 eggs, beaten
2 tablespoons sun-dried tomato purée
450 ml (¾ pint) tepid water
50 g (2 oz) Parmesan cheese, grated
50 g (2 oz) pitted olives, chopped
2 teaspoons chopped fresh oregano

Nutritional information:
Kcals 120 (502 kj) Protein 6 g Carb 16 g
Fat 3 g Saturated fat 1 g Fibre 2 g

1 Grease and line a 900-g (2-lb) loaf tin. Sift the polenta, flour and dried milk powder together into a large bowl and stir well to combine. Stir in the yeast, sugar and xanthan gum.

2 Place the eggs, sun-dried tomato purée and water in another bowl and mix together, then stir into the dry ingredients and combine to form a soft dough. Beat for 5 minutes, then stir in the remaining ingredients.

3 Spoon the mixture into the prepared tin, cover with a clean damp tea towel and leave in a warm place to rise for about 30 minutes, until the mixture is near the top of the tin. Place in a preheated oven, 180°C (350°F) Gas Mark 4, for about 45 minutes until brown and hollow when tapped. Remove the loaf from the oven and transfer to a wire rack to cool.

potato flat bread

A fairly dense bread, this is best served warm from the oven spread with butter.

Serves 12
Preparation time 15 minutes
Cooking time 35 minutes

150 g (5 oz) potato, chopped into 2-cm
   (¾-inch) cubes and cooked in boiling
   water for 10 minutes
300 ml (½ pint) milk, warmed
2 eggs, beaten
375 g (12 oz) brown rice flour
1 teaspoon xanthan gum
2 tablespoons olive oil
1 tablespoon gluten-free baking powder
pinch salt
2 teaspoons caster sugar

Nutritional information:
Kcals 65 (272 kj) Protein 2 g Carb 11 g
Fat 1 g Saturated fat 0 g Fibre 1 g

1 Grease a 23-cm (9-inch) square baking tin. Place the potato, milk and egg in a large bowl and beat together, then fold in the remaining ingredients.

2 Spoon the mixture into the prepared tin and place in a preheated oven, 200°C (400°F) Gas Mark 6, for 30–35 minutes, until golden and firm to the touch. Remove from the oven and leave to cool in the tin.

olive and sun-dried tomato scones

These can be knocked up in no time, so eat the same day while still warm from the oven.

Makes 8 scones
Preparation time 15 minutes
Cooking time 12 minutes

175 g (6 oz) rice flour
75 g (3 oz) potato flour
1 teaspoon xanthan gum
1 teaspoon gluten-free baking powder
1 teaspoon bicarbonate of soda
75 g (3 oz) butter, cubed
25 g (1 oz) pitted green olives, chopped
4 sun-dried tomatoes, chopped
1 tablespoon chopped fresh parsley
1 large egg, beaten
4 tablespoons buttermilk, plus a little
   extra for brushing

Nutritional information:
Kcals 198 (828 kj) Protein 5 g Carb 21 g
Fat 10 g Saturated fat 6 g Fibre 2 g

SHOWN ON PAGE 2

1 Place the flours, xanthan gum, baking powder, bicarbonate of soda and butter in a food processor and whiz until the mixture resembles fine breadcrumbs, or rub in by hand in a large bowl. Stir the olives, tomatoes and parsley into the mixture, then, using the blade of a knife, stir in the egg and buttermilk until the mixture comes together.

2 Tip the dough out on to a surface dusted lightly with rice flour and gently press it down to a thickness of 2.5 cm (1 inch). Use a 5-cm (2-inch) cutter to cut out the scones. Place on a lightly floured baking sheet, brush with a little buttermilk and place in a preheated oven, 220°C (425°F) Gas Mark 7, for about 12 minutes until golden and risen. Remove the scones from the oven and transfer to a wire rack to cool.

potato and thyme griddle scones

These light bites are best served warm with some cheese or butter.

Makes 6 scones
Preparation time 10 minutes
Cooking time 5 minutes

250 g (8 oz) potato, chopped into 2-cm (¾-inch) cubes and cooked in boiling water for 10 minutes
50 g (2 oz) rice flour, plus a little extra for dusting
pinch salt
1 teaspoon gluten-free baking powder
1 teaspoon fresh thyme, chopped
2 tablespoons buttermilk
1 egg, beaten
a little oil and butter for cooking

Nutritional information:
Kcals 91 (380 kj) Protein 1 g Carb 15 g
Fat 3 g Saturated fat 2 g Fibre 1 g

1 Place the potato and butter in a large bowl and mash together until smooth, then stir in the remaining ingredients until combined. Bring the mixture together to form a ball. Tip out on to a surface dusted lightly with rice flour, roll into a round about 5-mm (¼-inch) thick and cut into six triangles.

2 Brush a griddle or nonstick frying pan with a little oil and add a knob of butter, then cook the scones for a few minutes on each side until golden. Serve with butter and cheese for a delicious lunch.

caraway and sunflower-seed buns

Fill the kitchen with the fantastic aroma of caraway
when you make these tasty buns.

Makes 8 buns
Preparation time 25 minutes, plus
  proving
Cooking time 25 minutes

200 g (7 oz) buckwheat flour
200 g (7 oz) brown rice flour, plus a
  little extra for dusting
2 teaspoons xanthan gum
2 tablespoons dried milk powder
2 tablespoons sunflower seeds
2 teaspoons caraway seeds
7 g (¼ oz) sachet fast-action dried yeast
2 teaspoons sugar
300 ml (½ pint) warm water
2 eggs, beaten

for the glaze
1 egg, beaten
1 tablespoon milk
1 teaspoon caraway seeds

Nutritional information:
Kcals 220 (920 kj) Protein 7 g Carb 43 g
Fat 3 g Saturated fat 1 g Fibre 1 g

1 Place the flours, xanthan gum, dried milk powder, sunflower seeds and caraway seeds in a large bowl and mix together. Place the yeast, sugar and water in another bowl and stand it in a warm place for 15 minutes until frothy.

2 Pour the liquid over the dry ingredients with the beaten eggs and stir together to form a soft dough. Tip the dough out on to a surface dusted lightly with rice flour and knead for 5 minutes. Split the dough into eight pieces and make each into a bun shape. Place on a baking sheet, cover with a damp cloth and leave to prove for 40 minutes.

3 Mix together the egg and milk and brush this over the buns, then sprinkle a few caraway seeds on top. Place in a preheated oven, 200°C (400°F) Gas Mark 6, for 25 minutes until golden and hollow-sounding when tapped. Remove the buns from the oven and transfer to a wire rack to cool.

blue cheese and rosemary biscuits

These are like a delicious cheesy pastry – great with cheese after dinner.

Makes 20 biscuits
Preparation time 5 minutes, plus chilling
Cooking time 12 minutes

75 g (3 oz) Stilton cheese, crumbled
75 g (3 oz) butter, softened
100 g (3½ oz) rice flour
1 tablespoon polenta
1 teaspoon chopped fresh rosemary
1 egg yolk

Nutritional information:
Kcals 73 (305 kj) **Protein** 2 g **Carb** 3 g
Fat 5 g **Saturated fat** 4 g **Fibre** 0 g

1 Place all the ingredients except the egg yolk in a food processor and whiz until well combined, or beat in a large bowl. Add the egg yolk and whiz for a few seconds until the mixture comes together to form a soft dough.

2 Form the dough into a ball, then place it on a surface dusted lightly with rice flour and roll into a sausage shape about 15 cm (6 inches) long. Wrap closely and chill for half an hour.

3 Remove the dough from the refrigerator, unwrap and place on the floured surface. Slice the sausage into 20 discs, arrange on baking sheets and place in a preheated oven, 200°C (400°F) Gas Mark 6, for about 12 minutes until golden. Leave to cool on the baking sheets and then serve.

garlic and caramelized onion bhajis

These are great served with an Indian meal or filled
with your choice of filling.

Serves 6
Preparation 20 minutes
Cooking time 5 minutes

2 tablespoons olive oil
1 onion, sliced
2 garlic cloves, sliced
1 teaspoon cumin seeds
2 tablespoons chopped fresh coriander
200 g (7 oz) gram flour
1 teaspoon bicarbonate of soda
½ teaspoon salt
250 ml (8 fl oz) water

Nutritional information:
Kcals 310 (1296 kj) Protein 10 g Carb 60 g
Fat 5 g Saturated fat 01 g Fibre 0 g

1 Heat half the oil in a nonstick frying pan, add the onion, garlic
and cumin and fry for 5–6 minutes until golden and softened.
Stir through the coriander.

2 Meanwhile, mix together the flour, bicarbonate of soda, salt
and water and set aside for 10 minutes, then stir through the
onion mixture.

3 Heat a little of the remaining oil in the frying pan and add
spoonfuls of the mix, frying for 2–3 minutes, turning halfway
through cooking. Cook the remaining mix in the same way.

parmesan and paprika straws

These are very fragile but so tasty you won't be able to stop nibbling.

Makes 30
Preparation time 5 minutes, plus chilling
Cooking time 6 minutes

150 g (5 oz) rice flour
100 g (3½ oz) polenta
25 g (1 oz) Parmesan cheese, grated
1 teaspoon paprika
125 g (4 oz) butter
1 egg yolk
2 tablespoons milk

for the topping
1 tablespoon Parmesan cheese, grated

Nutritional information:
Kcals 63 (263 kj) Protein 1 g Carb 6 g
Fat 4 g Saturated fat 2 g Fibre 0 g

1 In a large bowl mix together the flour, polenta, Parmesan and paprika. Rub in the butter until the mixture resembles fine breadcrumbs.

2 Mix together the egg yolk and milk and add enough of the egg mixture to the dry ingredients to give a soft but not sticky dough. Form into a ball and chill for 30 minutes.

3 Roll out on a surface dusted lightly with rice flour to a rectangle approximately 2 mm (1/16 inch) thick, then cut into 30 strips. Place on a baking sheet and into a preheated oven, 200°C (400°F) Gas Mark 6, for 5–6 minutes until golden. Cool on the baking sheet, then carefully remove with a palette knife.

caramelized onion and feta biscuits

Onion and feta are great together in these crumbly biscuits.

Makes 20 biscuits
Preparation time 20 minutes, plus chilling
Cooking time 12 minutes

1 teaspoon olive oil
1 small onion, sliced
75 g (3 oz) butter
75 g (3 oz) feta cheese, crumbled
100 g (3½ oz) rice flour
1 tablespoon polenta
1 teaspoon chopped fresh thyme
1 egg yolk

Nutritional information:
Kcals 63 (263 kj) Protein 1 g Carb 3 g
Fat g 4 Saturated fat g Fibre 0 g

1 Heat the oil in a frying pan and fry the onion for 10 minutes until golden and soft. Meanwhile, place all the remaining ingredients except the egg yolk in a food processor and whiz until well combined, or beat in a large bowl. Add the egg yolk and whiz for a few seconds until the mixture comes together, then knead in the onion until well combined.

2 Form the dough into a ball, then place it on a surface dusted lightly with rice flour and roll into a sausage shape about 15 cm (6 inches) long. Wrap closely and chill for half an hour.

3 Remove the dough from the refrigerator, unwrap and place on the floured surface. Slice the sausage into 20 discs, arrange on baking sheets and place in a preheated oven, 200°C (400°F) Gas Mark 6, for about 12 minutes until golden. Leave to cool on the baking sheets for a few minutes, then transfer to a wire rack.

kids in the
kitchen

messy marshmallow krispies

Relive your childhood with these yummy yet oh-so-simple morsels.

Makes 12 cakes
Preparation time 5 minutes, plus chilling

150 g (5 oz) gluten-free milk chocolate
50 g (2 oz) gluten-free toffee
25 g (1 oz) butter
100 g (3½ oz) ready-to-eat dried
  apricots, chopped
handful mini marshmallows
75 g (3 oz) gluten-free crisped
  rice cereal

Nutritional information:
Kcals 122 (510 kj) Protein 2 g Carb 20 g
Fat 4 g Saturated fat 1 g Fibre 0 g

1 Line a baking sheet with greaseproof paper. Place the chocolate, toffee and butter in a heatproof bowl over a pan of simmering water and leave until melted.

2 Remove the pan from the heat, stir well, then mix in the remaining ingredients. Place spoonfuls of the mixture on the prepared baking sheet and leave until set.

toffee crackles

These chewy nutty treats are great for a children's party.

Makes 12 cakes
Preparation time 10 minutes, plus chilling

100 g (3½ oz) gluten-free toffee
75 g (3 oz) gluten-free crunchy peanut butter
75 g (3 oz) gluten-free milk chocolate
25 g (1 oz) butter
75 g (3 oz) gluten-free cornflakes

Nutritional information:
Kcals 144 (602 kj) Protein 3 g Carb 15 g
Fat 8 g Saturated fat 4 g Fibre 0 g

1 Place the toffee, peanut butter, chocolate and butter in a small saucepan over a low heat and cook for 2–3 minutes until melted.

2 Remove the pan from the heat and leave to cool for a few minutes, then stir in the cornflakes. Spoon the mixture into 12 paper cases and chill until firm.

orange animal biscuits

These crunchy tasty biscuits hold their shape well
when cooked and look fun once decorated.

Makes 20 biscuits
Preparation time 10 minutes
Cooking time 10 minutes

200 g (7 oz) brown rice flour
½ teaspoon xanthan gum
1 teaspoon gluten-free baking powder
50 g (2 oz) soft light brown sugar
grated rind 1 orange
50 g (2 oz) butter
1 egg
2 tablespoons golden syrup

for the decoration
150 g (5 oz) icing sugar
1 tablespoon boiling water
food colouring (optional)
gluten-free sweets (optional)

Nutritional information:
Kcals 106 (443 kj) Protein 0 g Carb 22 g
Fat 2 g Saturated fat 1 g Fibre 0 g

1 Place all the dry ingredients in a food processor, turn the motor on, then feed the remaining ingredients down the tube, adding a little extra flour if the mixture becomes too wet or adding a little milk if the mix is too dry.

2 Scrape the dough out of the bowl on to a surface dusted lightly with rice flour. Roll out the dough to a thickness of 5 mm (¼ inch) and use animal cutters of your choice to cut out 20 biscuits, rolling up any excess dough and rerolling and cutting again.

3 Place the biscuits on baking sheets and place in a preheated oven, 160°C (325°F) Gas Mark 3, for about 10 minutes until golden. Remove from the oven and transfer to a wire rack to cool.

4 Mix the icing sugar with the water and add colouring if you like. Smooth over the biscuits, or just use some to pipe on details, decorate with sweets, if using, then leave to set.

sticky gingerbread

Adding preserved ginger to the traditional recipe provides little jewels of surprise in this fab favourite.

Makes 16 pieces
Preparation time 10 minutes
Cooking time 45 minutes

300 g (10 oz) brown rice flour
50 g (2 oz) soft light brown sugar
1 teaspoon bicarbonate of soda
1 teaspoon ground ginger
100 g (3½ oz) butter
4 tablespoons black treacle
2 tablespoons golden syrup
2 pieces preserved ginger, finely
   chopped, plus 1 tablespoon of the
   syrup
150 ml (¼ pint) milk
1 egg, beaten

Nutritional information:
Kcals 139 (581 kj) Protein 2 g Carb 32 g
Fat 18 g Saturated fat 7 g Fibre 1 g

1 Grease and line a 20 x 15-cm (8 x 6-inch) cake tin. Place the flour, sugar, bicarbonate of soda and ground ginger in a large bowl and mix together.

2 Put the butter, treacle, syrup, preserved ginger and ginger syrup in a small saucepan and place it over a low heat until the butter has melted. Beat into the dry ingredients with the milk and egg and stir well.

3 Pour the mixture into the prepared tin and place in a preheated oven, 150°C (300°F) Gas Mark 2, for 40–45 minutes until firm to the touch. Cool, then cut into 16 squares. This keeps well for 3–4 days in an airtight tin.

fruity drop scones with butterscotch sauce

Making these little drop scones is so easy, and they are very moreish for children and adults alike!

Makes 12–14 scones
Preparation time 10 minutes
Cooking time 10 minutes

150 g (5 oz) brown rice flour
1 teaspoon gluten-free baking powder
8 tablespoons milk
2 eggs
50 g (2 oz) caster sugar
50 g (2 oz) raisins or dried cranberries
knob of butter, for frying

for the butterscotch sauce
4 tablespoons double cream
50 g (2 oz) butter
50 g (2 oz) soft light brown sugar
1 tablespoon honey

Nutritional information:
Kcals 166 (694 kj) Protein 2 g Carb 24 g
Fat 7 g Saturated fat 4 g Fibre 0 g

1 Place the flour, baking powder, milk, eggs and sugar in a bowl and whisk them together until smooth, then stir in the raisins. Set aside to rest.

2 Meanwhile, to make the butterscotch sauce, place all the ingredients in a small saucepan, bring to the boil and then simmer for 3 minutes.

3 Heat the butter in a heavy-based frying pan or skillet and add spoonfuls of the batter. Cook for about 1 minute until bubbles appear then turn over and cook for a further 20 seconds. Remove and keep warm on a plate while you continue with all the remaining batter, then serve drizzled with the butterscotch sauce.

victoria sandwich cake

This is a great everyday cake to which you can add flavours such as orange or lemon rind, if you like, or make a chocolate version for a birthday.

Serves 12
Preparation time 10 minutes
Cooking time 20 minutes

175 g (6 oz) butter, softened
175 g (6 oz) caster sugar
175 g (6 oz) brown rice flour
3 eggs
1 tablespoon gluten-free baking powder
few drops vanilla essence
1 tablespoon milk

for the decoration
4 tablespoons raspberry jam
icing sugar to dust

Nutritional information:
Kcals 253 (1058 kj) Protein 2 g Carb 32 g
Fat 13 g Saturated fat 8 g Fibre 0 g

1 Grease and flour two x 18-cm (7-inch) round nonstick cake tins. Place all the cake ingredients in a food processor and whiz until smooth, or beat in a large bowl.

2 Divide the mixture between the prepared tins and place in a preheated oven, 200°C (400°F) Gas Mark 6, for about 20 minutes until golden and risen. Remove the cakes from the oven and transfer to a wire rack to cool, then sandwich them together with the jam and dust with icing sugar.

Variation

For a scrumptious chocolate cake ideal for a birthday celebration try the following.

Make the cakes above, replacing 1 tablespoon of rice flour with cocoa powder. Make a chocolate icing by dissolving 2 tablespoons cocoa powder in 2 tablespoons boiling water and leaving to cool. Beat together 375 g (12 oz) icing sugar and 175 g (6 oz) softened butter until light and fluffy, then beat in the cocoa mixture. Use to fill and cover the cake.

melting chocolate bites

Light and fluffy, these little cakes are also good for dessert with a little gluten-free ice cream.

Makes 12 cakes
Preparation time 10 minutes
Cooking time 6 minutes

75 g (3 oz) gluten-free milk chocolate
100 g (3½ oz) butter
2 eggs
2 egg yolks
50 g (2 oz) caster sugar
1 tablespoon rice flour

Nutritional information:
Kcals 130 (543 kj) Protein 2 g Carb 8 g
Fat 10 g Saturated fat 6 g Fibre 0 g

1 Line a 12-hole mini-muffin tin with paper cases. Place the chocolate and butter in a heatproof bowl over a pan of simmering water and leave until melted.

2 In a separate bowl, whisk together the eggs, yolks and the sugar until thick and pale. Fold in the chocolate mixture and the flour, then pour the mixture into the paper cases. Place in a preheated oven, 200°C (400°F) Gas Mark 6, for 6 minutes. Remove the cakes from the oven and transfer to a wire rack to cool.

chocolate and fudge mini muffins

These scrummy mouthfuls contain everyone's favourite flavours.

Makes 40 muffins
Preparation time 30 minutes
Cooking time 15 minutes

200 g (7 oz) brown rice flour
2 tablespoons gram flour
1 teaspoon bicarbonate of soda
2 teaspoons gluten-free baking powder
½ teaspoon xanthan gum
125 g (4 oz) golden caster sugar
75 g (3 oz) butter, melted
1 egg, beaten
200 ml (7 fl oz) buttermilk
75 g (3 oz) gluten-free milk chocolate drops or chopped, gluten-free milk chocolate

for the fudge
397 g (13 oz) can condensed milk
150 ml (¼ pint) milk
500 g (1 lb) soft light brown sugar
100 g (3½ oz) butter

Nutritional information:
Kcals 71 (297 kj) Protein 0 g Carb 11 g
Fat 3 g Saturated fat 2 g Fibre 0 g

1 To make the fudge, place all the ingredients in a heavy-based saucepan and heat gently until the sugar has dissolved; bring to the boil and boil for about 10 minutes until the mixture reaches 116°C (230°F) on a sugar thermometer. Remove from the heat and beat for 5 minutes, then pour into a tin and set aside to cool.

2 Meanwhile, line four 12-hole mini-muffin tins with 40 paper cases. Sift the flours, bicarbonate of soda, baking powder and xanthan gum together into a large bowl, then stir in the sugar.

3 In a separate bowl, mix together the, butter, egg and buttermilk. Gently combine the dry and wet ingredients, and lightly fold 75 g (3 oz) of the fudge, roughly chopped, and the chocolate in to the mixture, stirring well.

4 Spoon the mixture into the paper cases and place in a preheated oven, 200°C (400°F) Gas Mark 6, for 15 minutes until golden and risen. Remove the cakes from the oven and transfer to a wire rack to cool. They are best eaten the same day.

fruity mango flapjacks

Chewy and fruity, these are great for school packed lunches.

Makes 12 pieces
Preparation time 10 minutes
Cooking time 30 minutes

100 g (3½ oz) soft light brown sugar
150 g (5 oz) butter
2 tablespoons golden syrup
200 g (7 oz) millet flakes
2 tablespoons mixed seeds, e.g.
   pumpkin and sunflower
75 g (3 oz) dried mango, roughly
   chopped

Nutritional information:
Kcals 219 (915 kj) Protein 3 g Carb 23 g
Fat 13 g Saturated fat 7 g Fibre 2 g

1 Place the sugar, butter and syrup in a heavy-based saucepan and heat until melted, then stir in the remaining ingredients.

2 Spoon the mixture into a 28 x 18-cm (11 x 7-inch) nonstick baking tin, press down lightly and place in a preheated oven, 150°C (300°F) Gas Mark 2, for 30 minutes. Mark into 12 bars, then cool before removing from the tin.

marble cake squares

Vanilla and chocolate are common choices for a marble cake but food colouring also looks great!

Makes 16 pieces
Preparation time 10 minutes
Cooking time 25 minutes

175 g (6 oz) butter, softened
175 g (6 oz) caster sugar
100 g (3½ oz) brown rice flour
75 g (3 oz) maize/cornflour
3 eggs
1 tablespoon gluten-free
 baking powder
few drops vanilla essence
1 tablespoon milk
1 tablespoon cocoa powder

Nutritional information:
Kcals 179 (748 kj) Protein 1 g Carb 21 g
Fat 10 g Saturated fat 6 g Fibre 0 g

1 Grease and flour an 18-cm (7-inch) square cake tin. Place all the ingredients except the cocoa in a food processor and whiz until smooth, or beat in a large bowl.

2 Divide the mixture in two and beat the cocoa powder (or some food colouring) into one half. Spoon the mixes into a bowl and give a very gentle swirl, then spoon into the prepared tin.

3 Place in a preheated oven, 200°C (400°F) Gas Mark 6, for 25 minutes or until just firm to the touch. Remove the cake from the oven, leave to cool in the tin, then cut into 16 squares.

white choc drops

These biscuits are so melt-in-the-mouth
they won't last long!

Makes 20 biscuits
Preparation time 10 minutes, plus
   chilling
Cooking time 20 minutes

50 g (2 oz) white vegetable fat
50 g (2 oz) butter
50 g (2 oz) caster sugar
1 egg yolk
200 g (7 oz) brown rice flour, plus
   extra for dusting
1 tablespoon ground almonds
50 g (2 oz) gluten-free white chocolate,
   grated

Nutritional information:
Kcals 98 (410 kj) Protein 0 g Carb 13 g
Fat 5 g Saturated fat 3 g Fibre 0 g

1 Place the fats and sugar in a large bowl and beat together, then beat in the egg yolk followed by the remaining ingredients. Form the dough into a ball, wrap closely and chill for 1 hour.

2 Remove the dough from the refrigerator, unwrap and place on a surface dusted lightly with rice flour. Knead the dough a little to soften it, then divide into 20 balls.

3 Place the balls on two baking sheets, flatten them slightly with a fork and place in a preheated oven, 180°C (350°F) Gas Mark 4, for about 20 minutes until golden. Remove the biscuits from the oven and transfer to a wire rack to cool.

passion cake squares

Deliciously moist and full of wonderful flavours – what could be nicer?

Makes 16 pieces
Preparation time 10 minutes
Cooking time 1 hour

175 g (6 oz) brown rice flour
375 g (12 oz) caster sugar
2 teaspoons gluten-free baking powder
1 teaspoon xanthan gum
1 teaspoon ground cinnamon
150 ml (¼ pint) rapeseed or corn oil
2 eggs, beaten
few drops vanilla extract
375 g (12 oz) carrots, grated
50 g (2 oz) desiccated coconut
100 g (3½ oz) canned crushed
  pineapple, drained
50 g (2 oz) sultanas

for the topping
200 g (7 oz) cream cheese
2 tablespoons runny honey
75 g (3 oz) walnuts, chopped (optional)

Nutritional information:
Kcals 307 (1,283 kj) Protein 2 g Carb 27 g
Fat 21 g Saturated fat 7 g Fibre 1 g

1 Grease and flour a 20-cm (8-inch) square cake tin. Sift the flour, sugar, baking powder, xanthan gum and cinnamon together into a large bowl. Add the oil, eggs and vanilla extract and beat well.

2 Fold in the carrots, coconut, pineapple and sultanas and spoon the mixture into the prepared tin. Place in a preheated oven, 180°C (350°F) Gas Mark 4, for about 1 hour or until a skewer inserted in the middle comes out clean. Remove from the oven and cool in the tin.

3 Beat together the cream cheese and honey, and smooth over the cake then sprinkle the nuts, if using, on top. Cut into 16 squares.

gingerbread men

A chapter for children would be incomplete without these friendly spicy characters!

Makes 6 gingerbread men
Preparation time 15 minutes
Cooking time 10 minutes

150 g (5 oz) brown rice flour
2 tablespoons cornflour
pinch bicarbonate of soda
1 teaspoon ground ginger
½ teaspoon xanthan gum
40 g (1½ oz) butter
25 g (1 oz) soft light brown sugar
2 tablespoons golden syrup

for the decoration
100 g (3½ oz) gluten-free white
   chocolate, melted
gluten-free sweets or raisins (optional)

Nutritional information:
Kcals 169 (706 kj) **Protein** 0 g **Carb** 31 g
Fat 6 g **Saturated fat** 4 g **Fibre** 0 g

SHOWN ON PAGES 116–117

1 Sift all the dry ingredients together into a large bowl. Place the butter, sugar and syrup in a small saucepan and heat gently until melted, then stir into the flour mix and bring together to form a ball.

2 Place the dough on to a surface dusted lightly with rice flour and roll it out to a thickness of 5 mm (¼ inch). Cut out six gingerbread men or other shapes (depending on their size) with a cutter, then place on a baking sheet and place in a preheated oven, 190°C (375°F) Gas Mark 5, for 8–10 minutes until golden brown. Remove from the oven and transfer to a wire rack to cool.

3 Use the white chocolate to pipe features, such as buttons, on to the biscuits and decorate with sweets or raisins if desired.

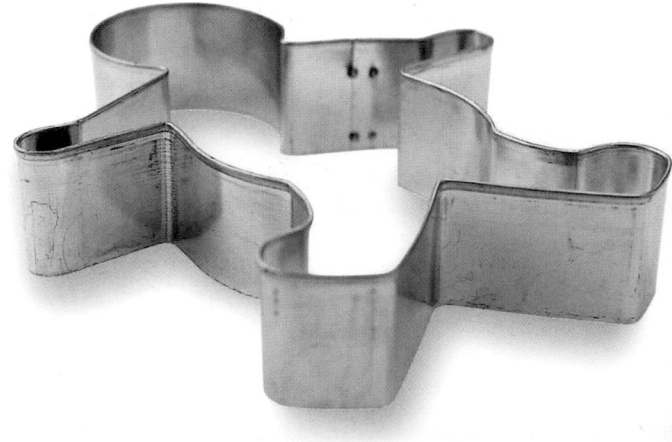

flower fairy cakes

Encourage the children to get artistic with decorating these scrumptious cakes.

Makes 12 cakes
Preparation time 10 minutes
Cooking time 20 minutes

1 tablespoon milk
125 g (4 oz) caster sugar
100 g (3½ oz) butter, softened
100 g (3½ oz) rice flour
1 tablespoon chickpea/gram flour
2 eggs, beaten
2 tablespoons ground almonds
1 teaspoon gluten-free baking powder
1 teaspoon xanthan gum
few drops vanilla essence

for the decoration
200 g (7 oz) icing sugar
1 tablespoon boiling water
coloured icing (those that are pre-made
  in tubes are great)

Nutritional information:
Kcals 227 (949 kj) Protein 1 g Carb 36 g
Fat 9 g Saturated fat 5 g Fibre 0 g

1 Line a 12-hole bun tin with paper cases. Place all the cake ingredients in a food processor and whiz until smooth, or beat in a large bowl.

2 Divide the mixture between the cases and place in a preheated oven, 200°C (400°F) Gas Mark 6, for 20 minutes until golden and risen. Remove the cakes from the oven and transfer to a wire rack to cool while making the icing.

3 Mix the icing sugar with the water and beat to give a smooth paste. Spread this over the cakes, then decorate with the coloured icing in flower designs.

cheese, corn and bacon snack muffins

You could make these in mini-muffin size too –
perfect for a savoury snack or as part of a meal.

Makes 12 muffins
Preparation time 10 minutes
Cooking time 20 minutes

100 g (3½ oz) brown rice flour
50 g (2 oz) maize/cornflour
2 teaspoons gluten-free baking powder
1 teaspoon xanthan gum
100 g (3½ oz) polenta
2 eggs
75 g (3 oz) butter, melted
200 ml (7 fl oz) buttermilk
75 g (3 oz) canned sweetcorn, drained
50 g (2 oz) bacon, grilled and chopped
2 tablespoons grated Parmesan cheese
pinch salt
100 g (3½ oz) Cheddar cheese, cut into
   12 cubes

Nutritional information:
Kcals 160 (669 kj) Protein 5 g Carb 14 g
Fat 9 g Saturated fat 6 g Fibre 0 g

1 Line a large 12-hole muffin tray with muffin cases. Place all the dry ingredients in a large bowl and stir them together. Place the eggs, melted butter and buttermilk in another bowl and mix them together, then stir this mixture into the dry ingredients with the corn, bacon, Parmesan and salt.

2 Spoon half the mixture into the muffin cases, add a cube of Cheddar, then spoon the remaining mixture on top. Place in a preheated oven, 180°C (350°F) Gas Mark 4, for 20 minutes until risen and golden. These are best eaten on the same day.

date and apple crumble tops

These moist sponges have a delicious crunchy crumb topping.

Makes 12 cakes
Preparation time 15 minutes
Cooking time 15 minutes

150 g (5 oz) butter, softened
150 g (5 oz) granulated sugar
75 g (3 oz) rice flour
75 g (3 oz) maize/cornflour
1 tablespoon gluten-free baking powder
2 tablespoons milk
3 eggs, beaten
2 eating apples, peeled, cored and chopped
75 g (3 oz) ready-to-eat dried dates

for the topping
pinch ground mixed spice
3 tablespoons brown rice flour
3 tablespoons demerara sugar
2 tablespoons butter
50 g (2 oz) walnuts, roughly chopped
1 tablespoon water

Nutritional information:
Kcals 265 (1,108 kj) Protein 3 g Carb 27 g
Fat 16 g Saturated fat 9 g Fibre 0 g

1 Line a 12-hole bun tin with paper cases. Place the butter, sugar, flours, baking powder, milk and eggs in a food processor and whiz until well combined, or beat in a large bowl. Fold the apple and dates in, then spoon the mixture into the paper cases.

2 To make the topping, place the spice, flour, sugar and butter in a bowl and rub in using your fingertips. Stir in the walnuts and water and bring the mixture together, then sprinkle it over the top of the cakes.

3 Place in a preheated oven, 200°C (400°F) Gas Mark 6, for 15 minutes until golden and just firm to the touch. Remove the cakes from the oven and leave to cool.

popcorn clusters

Kids will love helping with these yummy treats,
especially scraping the bowl afterwards!

Makes 24 cakes
Preparation time 5 minutes, plus chilling

1 teaspoon oil
2 tablespoons popping corn
50 g (2 oz) butter
1 tablespoon golden syrup
200 g (7 oz) gluten-free milk chocolate
50 g (2 oz) unsalted peanuts, roughly
   chopped (optional)

Nutritional information:
Kcals 114 (477 kj) Protein 2 g Carb 8 g
Fat 8 g Saturated fat 3 g Fibre 0 g

1 Heat the oil in a large saucepan. Add the corn, then cover with a lid and shake the pan and soon the corn will start popping. Carry on shaking until the popping stops, then remove from the heat.

2 Place the butter, syrup and chocolate in a saucepan and melt over gentle heat, then stir this into the popcorn with the peanuts, if using. Spoon the mixture into 24 paper cases and leave to set in the refrigerator.

pizza scrolls

You can use any topping to suit your taste or whatever you have in the refrigerator.

Makes 8 pieces
Preparation time 25 minutes, plus proving
Cooking time 15 minutes

2 x 7 g (¼ oz) sachets fast-action dried yeast
1 teaspoon caster sugar
250 ml (8 fl oz) milk, warmed
175 g (6 oz) rice flour, plus extra for dusting
125 g (4 oz) potato flour
1 teaspoon gluten-free baking powder
1 teaspoon xanthan gum
pinch salt
1 tablespoon sunflower oil
1 egg, beaten

for the filling
4 tablespoons passata
200 g (7 oz) grated mixed cheese, e.g. mozzarella and Cheddar
75 g (3 oz) wafer-thin ham, shredded
handful fresh basil, chopped

Nutritional information:
Kcals 331 (1384 kj) Protein 12 g Carb 48 g
Fat 11 g Saturated fat 8 g Fibre 1 g

1 Place the yeast, sugar and the milk in a bowl and set aside for about 10 minutes until frothy. In a large bowl stir together the flours, baking powder, xanthan gum and the salt.

2 Mix the oil and egg into the yeast mixture and pour this into the flour mixture, using a fork to bring the mixture together. Tip it out on to a surface dusted lightly with rice flour and knead for 5 minutes, adding a little flour if the mixture becomes sticky. Place in a lightly oiled bowl, cover with a damp cloth and leave to rise in a warm place for about 40 minutes or until well risen.

3 Roll the dough out on the floured surface to a rectangle approximately 30 x 25 cm (12 x 10 inches), spread with the passata, then sprinkle over the other toppings. Roll the pizza up from one long edge, then slice into eight pieces.

4 Place the rolled-up pizza scrolls side by side on a lightly oiled heavy baking sheet or tin. They should be pushed up against each other so the sides are touching. Place in a preheated oven, 220°C (425°F) Gas Mark 7, for 12–15 minutes until golden. Eat warm from the oven, one or two scrolls per child, depending on appetite.

index

a

almonds
  apricot almond crunch biscuits 88
  blackberry and almond cake 64
  moist almond cake 49
apples
  blueberry and apple cake 40
  date and apple crumble tops 138
  fudgy apple loaf 44
apricots
  apricot almond crunch biscuits 88
  white chocolate and apricot muffins 21

b

bacon: cheese, corn and bacon snack muffins 136
Bakewell slice 78
banana and date bread 57
banoffee bites 37
beetroot speckle cake 56
blackberry and almond cake 64
blueberry and apple cake 40
buckwheat bread 103
butterscotch
  butterscotch layer cake 48
  fruity drop scones with butterscotch sauce 123

c

caraway and sunflower-seed buns 110
carrot cake with passion-fruit topping 60
cheese
  blue cheese and rosemary biscuits 111
  caramelized onion and feta biscuits 115
  cheese, corn and bacon snack muffins 136
  cherry and ricotta cake 65
  feta and herb loaf 96
  Parmesan, olive and sun-dried tomato loaf 104
  Parmesan and paprika straws 114
cherries
  cherry crumble muffins 27
  cherry and ricotta cake 65
chestnut purée/spread:
  chocolate and chestnut roulade 46
chocolate
  chewy nutty chocolate brownies 74
  chocolate caramel shortbread 70
  chocolate and chestnut roulade 46
  chocolate chip cookies 86
  chocolate courgette muffins 24
  chocolate and fudge mini muffins 127
  chocolate hazelnut cake 41
  chocolate and rum cake 50
  espresso and white chocolate brownies 73
  hazelnut and chocolate macaroons 76
  melting chocolate bites 126
  pistachio and choc chip shortbread 80
  white choc drops 131
  white chocolate and apricot muffins 21
coconut
  coconut buns 29
  coconut macaroons 68
  coconut and mango cake 42
coeliac disease 8–9
coffee
  espresso cream gâteau 53
  espresso and white chocolate brownies 73
corn bread 99
courgettes: chocolate courgette muffins 24
cranberry and orange cupcakes 25
cream: espresso cream gâteau 53

d

dates
  banana and date bread 57
  date and apple crumble tops 138
  date and pecan muffins 17

f

flour 10
flower fairy cakes 135
fudge: chocolate and fudge mini muffins 127

g

garlic and caramelized onion bhajis 113
ginger
  crisp ginger biscuits 89
  gingerbread men 134
  sticky gingerbread 122
gluten 8
  gluten-free baking 10–13
  intolerance 9
guar gum 13

h

hazelnuts
  chocolate hazelnut cake 41
  hazelnut and chocolate macaroons 76
  hazelnut meringue stack 62

herbs: feta and herb loaf 96
honey: orange and honey
cake 45

l
lavender fairy cakes 18
lemons
lemon drizzle loaf 54
lemon madeleines 69
lemon, pistachio and
fruit squares 83
lemon and raspberry
cupcakes 22
lemony poppets 84
pistachio and citrus sand
cake 61

m
mangoes
coconut and mango cake
42
fruity mango flapjacks
128
marble cake squares 130
marshmallows: messy
marshmallow krispies
118
marzipan: pear and
marzipan loaf 52
mincemeat: bite-sized
mince pies 33

n
nuts
chewy nutty chocolate
brownies 74
nutty seed loaf 100
see also under individual nut

o
olives
olive and sun-dried
tomato scones 107
Parmesan, olive and sun-
dried tomato loaf 104
onions
caramelized onion and
feta biscuits 115
garlic and caramelized
onion bhajis 113
oranges
cranberry and orange
cupcakes 25
moist orange buns 32
orange and honey cake
45
orange and pistachio
butterfly cakes 16
orange and polenta
crispy cookies 90
orange animal biscuits
120
pistachio and citrus sand
cake 61

p
paprika: Parmesan and
paprika straws 114
passion-fruit: carrot cake
with passion-fruit
topping 60
peanuts: peanutty squares
81
pears: pear and marzipan
loaf 52
pecans
date and pecan muffins
17
perfect pecan pies 34

pineapple: passion cake
squares 133
pistachios
lemon, pistachio and
fruit squares 83
orange and pistachio
butterfly cakes 16
pistachio and choc chip
shortbread 80
pistachio and citrus sand
cake 61
pizza scrolls 140
plums
plum and polenta
muffins 20
plum pastries 77
polenta
orange and polenta
crispy cookies 90
plum and polenta
muffins 20
popcorn clusters 139
potatoes
potato and thyme griddle
scones 108
potato flat bread 106
pumpkin loaf 98

r
raisins: fruity drop scones
with butterscotch sauce
123
raspberries: lemon and
raspberry cupcakes 22
rice cereal: messy
marshmallow krispies 118
rosemary: blue cheese and
rosemary biscuits 111
rum: chocolate and rum
cake 50

s
seeds: nutty seed loaf 100
soda bread 95
strawberries: scrumptious
strawberry scones 30
sunflower seeds: caraway
and sunflower-seed buns
110
sweetcorn: cheese, corn and
bacon snack muffins 136

t
thyme: potato and thyme
griddle scones 108
tiramisu cupcakes 28
toffee
banoffee bites 37
toffee crackles 119
tomatoes
olive and sun-dried
tomato scones 107
Parmesan, olive and sun-
dried tomato loaf 104
tropical fruit cake 59

v
Victoria sandwich 124

w
walnuts
walnut biscuits 85
walnut loaf 102
white loaf 94

x
xanthan gum 10

acknowledgements

Thanks to my husband, Phil, the boys, Ollie and Freddie, and my willing neighbours for sampling all of the recipes and giving their positive responses.

Executive Editor: Nicola Hill
Editor: Lisa John
Executive Art Editor: Penny Stock
Designer: Miranda Harvey
Photographer: Emma Neish
Home Economist: Felicity Barnum-Bobb
Production Controller: Manjit Sihra